Ebenezer Prout

Madagascar

Its Mission and its Martyrs

Ebenezer Prout

Madagascar
Its Mission and its Martyrs

ISBN/EAN: 9783337060138

Printed in Europe, USA, Canada, Australia, Japan

Cover: Foto ©ninafisch / pixelio.de

More available books at **www.hansebooks.com**

MADAGASCAR:

ITS MISSION AND ITS MARTYRS.

LONDON:
PRINTED BY W. STEVENS, FOR THE
LONDON MISSIONARY SOCIETY.

MDCCCLXIII.

PREFACE

TO THE SECOND EDITION.

THE present issue is not designed to supersede the First Edition of this work. In preparing that edition, the object of the Compiler was to produce a small volume, in an inexpensive form. With this view, he endeavoured to compress the most interesting events in the history of Madagascar during the last forty-two years into the narrowest space compatible with perspicuity. The same design required the use of a smaller type and a closer page than could have been desired. These disadvantages disappear in the present volume. But the most important difference between the two issues will be found in additional facts and documents received since the publication of the First Edition.

E. PROUT.

MISSION HOUSE, BLOMFIELD STREET,
January, 1863.

Madagascar. It is my firm opinion that it is impossible for any one to feel the full force of this impression, unless he has witnessed and studied it himself. The effect of Christian teaching in Madagascar struck me as possessing a most remarkable character."

Of this work the present volume contains an outline, with numerous incidents which strikingly indicate its Divine origin. More than this it would have been unwise to attempt, within limits so restricted. The documents and details which belong to the history of the first twenty years of the Mission, must therefore be sought in the admirable works of the Rev. W. Ellis, and Messrs. Freeman and Johns. But although the following pages contain merely a concise sketch of the progress and effects of Christianity in Madagascar during the protracted period of persecution now so happily terminated, it is believed that such a narrative is urgently required; that, considering the previous condition of those whose faith and patience it describes, more marvellous illustrations of the operation of "the word of truth" and "the power of God" are not to be found in the history of the Church; and that no Christians present a stronger claim to confidence and love, and no Mission more deserves generous support.

MADAGASCAR:

ITS MISSION AND ITS MARTYRS.

UNTIL within a comparatively recent period, few countries of equal extent and importance have attracted less attention or awakened less interest than Madagascar. With an area larger than that of Great Britain and Ireland combined; unusually rich in mineral treasures and vegetable productions; fitted by its position, climate, soil, and harbours, to become wealthy and powerful; and capable, moreover, of supporting a population manyfold greater than the four millions by which it is now inhabited, this fine island would have been scarcely missed from the map of the world, had its name been expunged at the beginning of the present century. But forty years ago, Philanthropists and Christians hailed with gladness the commencement of a new era in its history; and bright indeed did that era promise to become. Its dawn was as a morning without clouds. But, alas! it proved as brief as it was bright. Portentous darkness soon followed, and at length a storm burst, which for nearly thirty years desolated the land. Great indeed was the grief of those who had laboured for the salvation of its inhabitants, when, driven from its shores, they heard from afar the wail of sorrow and the cry for help. And the pain thus produced became more acute as years rolled on, and fragments of intelligence —at long intervals—reached them, which revealed the character of the sufferers and the extent of their sufferings. Christian sympathy had place in many hearts, and the prayer arose from many lips, "Lord, how long shall the wicked triumph?" And once and again it was believed that that prayer had been heard. The clouds seemed to open, and gleams of brightness to break through them. But they "returned after the rain." Hope, thus long deferred and often disappointed, made the heart sick. Supplications, indeed, were still made to God continually, and many a weary watcher looked out with sad and sorrowful thoughts upon the darkness, and longed for day. Thanks be to God! the day has at length dawned—and that, too, with no hazy indistinctness, no shadowy forebodings of another storm. And what should add to the joy with which we mark the change is the fact, now so clearly revealed, that while the darkness prevailed, the sun above it was not merely shining on, but rising higher, and attaining the lofty altitude from which he is now flooding hill and valley, city and village, with beams far brighter than those of his early rising. These changes it is the object of the following pages very briefly to describe.

The history of the Madagascar Mission is comprehended within a period of rather more than forty years. It dates from 1820, when Missionaries from the London Missionary Society commenced their labours at Antananarivo, the capital. The necessity for such a movement, however, had been felt by the Directors from the formation of the Society. At the close of the last century, when Dr. Vanderkemp was departing for South Africa, they instructed him to ascertain the practicability of establishing a Mission in Madagascar. Subsequently the Rev. John Campbell, their African deputation, and the Rev. W. Milne, who was to visit Mauritius on his way to China, were charged with a similar commission. But although for nearly fifteen years the Directors ardently desired the evangelization of this fine island, and were prepared to make the attempt with vigour and liberality, it was not until 1814 that the first direct movement was made for its attainment. In that year, the Rev. J. Le Brun was sent to Mauritius, chiefly for the purpose of obtaining information, and adopting measures with a view to the establishment of a Mission in Madagascar. The result was, that in the autumn of 1818, Messrs. Bevan and Jones commenced their labours at Tamatave. But the climate of the country was then imperfectly understood; and the devoted brethren scarcely suspected that during the rainy season a dead and silent sea of malaria girdled the coast. This ignorance proved most fatal. In a short time, malignant fever had consigned Mr. and Mrs. Bevan, Mrs. Jones and two children, to the grave, while Mr. Jones, with broken health and bleeding heart, was compelled to return to Mauritius. It was suspected that they had been the victims of poison, but no sufficient grounds exist for such a surmise.

After recruiting his health at Mauritius, Mr. Jones, accompanied by James Hastie, Esq., the British resident, returned to Madagascar. But he had learned wisdom by painful experience. He resolved, therefore, not again to attempt to labour on the coast, but to proceed to the capital, which occupies a high and healthy position in the centre of the island. On his arrival he was cordially welcomed by the King, whose confidence and favour he soon secured by the simplicity and sincerity of his speech and actions, and whose countenance was readily given to his Missionary plans and proceedings. During the following year, the Rev. D. Griffiths and two Missionary artizans joined Mr. Jones at Antananarivo.

In 1822 the Rev. J. Jeffries and four other labourers followed, and entered with energy and hope upon their work. But their early difficulties were great. They had everything to learn and almost everything to teach. The people were somewhat acquainted with the mechanical arts, but they had not that indispensable instrument of social progress—a written language. The first Missionaries had, therefore, to learn by the ear alone, and to catch and record as they best could, the unfamiliar and uncouth words and phrases which came rushing from the lips of the natives. For some time, their labours were almost necessarily confined to the schools and the children; but as, hitherto, the Malagasy knew little of Europeans, except as slave-dealers, many of the parents regarded the proceedings of the Missionaries with suspicion, not unmixed with fear for the safety of their little ones. The King, however, early discerned the secular advantages which he and his people would derive from their instructions, and from the first he gave them his encouragement and aid. He sent the sons of his highest nobles to be taught, and took a pleasure in visiting the school, that he might hear them recite their lessons and sing their hymns. Soon the children, to many of whom the daily task was a most pleasant occupation, became much attached to their teachers and to the school. Often, indeed, before daybreak, as if impatient to begin their work, would groups of them gather outside the teacher's house, repeating the multiplication-table, or other prescribed exercises in which they were interested. An unexpected and amusing proof of their fondness for the school occurred not long after its commencement. Requiring some relaxation for themselves, and believing that Malagasy children, like British youth, would be gratified with a holiday, one day the announcement was made that the school would be closed for a short time. This extraordinary announcement gave rise to much speculation on the part of the parents, but the only explanation they could devise was, that the Missionaries intended this as a punishment for some unknown offence of their children. A *kabary*, or public council, was consequently summoned to investigate the matter, and even the King sent to inquire what evil the pupils had done. Of course the explanation was as satisfactory to the parents, as their anxiety for the improvement of the children was encouraging to the Missionaries.

But although, at first, before native assistants had been trained, the Missionaries were compelled to devote much of their attention to the schools, no opportunity was lost, either by them or by the Christian artizans, for teaching and preaching the Gospel. As soon, moreover, as they had acquired some familiarity with the language, they began a translation of the New Testament and the preparation of other works of instruction; and when, after some years, printing-presses were set up, the wonder and delight of the people were almost unbounded. The rapidity with which the young and those adults who had felt anything of the influence of religion, learned to read, caused a demand for books far beyond the supply. This was especially the case with the Scriptures, the desire to possess which was very strong. Of this, a single illustration must suffice. Two young persons came to the Missionary, one of them a respectable female, with a slate in her hand, which she presented to him, with the following note written upon it:—

"I have long lived in darkness, and now desire to be brought into the light, that I may know about God, and his Son Jesus Christ. Oh! pity me! Have compassion upon me! Give me a copy of the New Testament! I am greatly in need of it. Be merciful to me, and grant me my request, if you possibly can!"

The increasing supply of books, now of all treasures the most precious in the estimation of many, proved not only a satisfaction to those who could read, but a strong stimulus to others to learn. Thus the demand for instruction spread, and the number of schools, both in the capital and in the country, increased so rapidly, that a general superintendence of them was all that the Missionaries could give; and, happily, more was not necessary. Many of the young people had by this time become qualified to teach others; and fortunate were they esteemed who were elevated to this service. Thus, when a new school was opened, many eager candidates competed for the post of teacher; and though these were not always Christians in the highest sense, they were familiar with the Scriptures, and had learned to despise the idols and superstitions of their country. In this way schools were founded in nearly a hundred principal villages. "These schools," to use the words of one of the Missionaries, "were filled with the choice youth of the country." As, however, for some time after their formation, there were no printed books, and the teachers were comparatively unfurnished, they were accustomed to return at certain periods to the capital that they might replenish their nearly exhausted stock of knowledge. But so anxious were they to teach, and so eager were their pupils to learn, that notwithstanding all their disadvantages, their educational progress was great and rapid.

The effect of the education thus wide-spread, was soon apparent. The taught imbibed the sentiments and manifested the spirit of the teachers. Nor was it surprising that a change so great should provoke resentment and resistance. One day, the headman of a village in which stood the shrine of a popular idol heard that the teacher had spoken of it with contempt. In a great rage, the petty chieftain hurried off to the school and charged the young man with the crime.

The teacher at once acknowledged it, adding that the idol was nothing, and of less use than the mere dust of the ground. A heavy blow from the heathen was the only answer which the brave youth received. Nor were the children much more respectful to the gods than their instructors. In one place a hailstorm had damaged the crops, which the heathen attributed to the insults offered by the children to the deities, and which they threatened to avenge, unless they were treated with greater reverence. But as "young Madagascar" was not to be scared and silenced by hard words and angry blows, their parents spoke of complaining to the King, and added with sorrow, "We have nursed you, and brought you up until this day; but now you forsake the customs of your forefathers." "We cannot," replied the children, "prevent your complaining to the King, but we have been taught to tell the truth; and if, to please you, we should say with our lips that we believe in the idol, while yet in our hearts we cannot do so, we should only lie." In despair of bringing back their children to the point from which they had now drifted far away by any influence of their own, the parents went to Radama, and in tones of bitter complaint cried, "Our children are forsaking the customs of our ancestors, and our gods," ascribing the change to the schools. But the King was too wise to interpose; so he quietly dismissed them with the admonition, "Do you mind your work, and let the children mind their lessons."

But the Missionaries were concerned that both teacher and taught should not only possess "the form of knowledge and of truth," but that they should feel its power. With this view they held meetings for special prayer, which many of the young regularly attended, and in which some of them took a public part, pouring out, in simple but earnest petitions, desires which the Missionaries believed God had inspired in their hearts.

As this volume is not designed to furnish a circumstantial narrative of the origin of the Madagascar Mission, or of its early progress, we shall merely add that, at the end of eight years from the settlement of Mr. Jones at Antananarivo, there were four thousand young people under Christian instruction, many of them children of the most powerful nobles in the land, some of whom subsequently brought forth the ripened fruits of the cultivation they now received.

But while education was thus spreading, large congregations statedly listened to the Gospel; Bible Classes had been formed, a Church was gathered, a considerable portion of the Scriptures, with many Christian books, was printed, and a feeling in favour of the new religion had spread far, and was constantly spreading farther in the city and through the surrounding province of Imerina.

Up to this point of their history, therefore, there was much of the bright and the fair in the prospects of the Missionaries. Nevertheless, their sky had been far from cloudless. Many occurrences had caused grief, and awakened anxiety. Once and again death had visited their little circle. The King, though their friend, and favourable to many of their proceedings, had no sympathy with their spiritual design; indeed, it was obvious that the requirements of the Gospel were his aversion. He was accustomed to say, "My book is within my own breast." But it was manifest that the moral intuitions of this pagan advocate, like those of some professedly Christian philosopher, were not "from above;" and if he cared but little for the idols, he probably cared still less for the Gospel. He even expressed the fear that the Missionaries were moving onwards too fast, and that the people were going too far from the customs of their ancestors. He moreover delighted in war, and when provoked, could show how much of the savage there was still in him. The people, too, were mostly heathen. Nor were the spiritual results, as yet, very abundant. These and other discouragements moderated the joy with which the Missionaries reaped the first fruits of their labour, and surveyed on every side the early promise of a far larger ingathering.

But at the time of which we write (1828) Radama died, when only thirty-six years of age. The Missionaries felt the loss to be that of a protector and friend. But at first they had no dark forebodings of the future. The rightful heir to the vacant throne was an excellent youth, named Rakotobe, who had been their first pupil, and in whose heart they believed there was some good thing towards the Lord God of Israel. Under his government they felt assured that their labours would have the widest scope, and the most enlightened encouragement. Rakotobe's father's name was Rataffe. This prince visited England in 1821, and was a mild and excellent man. His mother, too, was Radama's eldest sister. Nobody, therefore, could justly question his title to the throne, and it was generally expected that he would ascend it in peace. But this was not to be.

Radama had twelve wives. None of these were entitled to reign; but the eldest, Ranavalona, who had been the youngest wife of Radama's father, resolved to grasp the sceptre as it fell from her husband's hand. She was a bold, bad woman, with strong purpose and no principle. Though well aware that she could only gain her object by crime, she was ready to dare and to do the worst. With this view she drew a few men, as reckless and as wicked as herself, into the plot, promising, no doubt, high offices and large rewards as the recompense of their villany. But how could she attain the desired eminence? Murder was the sole means. The throne could only be reached over the slaughtered bodies of the rightful heir and his loyal adherents; but for all this she was prepared. After four nobles had been speared in the palace for asserting the claim of Rakotobe, armed men were sent to his residence near the capital to seize him ere the shadow of coming danger could fall upon his path. And as if death were not all that the murderess desired, the cruel instruments of her ambition dug the prince's grave before his eyes. While they were thus engaged, the pious youth kneeled down to pray, and in that attitude was pierced by the executioners' spears. Soon afterwards, his father and mother met the same fate, the latter having been starved to death. Ratafikia, Radama's brother, after lingering in agony eight days, in like manner perished. Then Rakatobe's grandmother and other relations were cut down by the Queen's ruthless orders, until all who were likely to oppose her usurpation had been destroyed. Thus did Ranavalona become the Sovereign of Madagascar. It was a beginning which agreed but too well with her long reign of darkness and terror, tyranny, persecution, and crime. Of this we shall meet with too many appalling details as we proceed—details which would have no place here but for the fact that, side by side with them, and in contrast with the usurper's deeds of cruelty and blood, stand forth a glorious array of Christian confessors and martyrs, together with evidences of the progress and the power of the religion for which they suffered, few parallels to which will be found in the history of the Church. In that contrast we shall see, as we proceed with our wondrous tale, one reason, at least, why He who sitteth in the heavens permitted the heathen to rage, and this sanguinary ruler to imagine so vain a thing against the Lord and against his Anointed, as to say, " Let us break their bonds asunder, and cast away their cords from us."

The feelings of the Missionaries, when they heard that Ranavalona reigned, and became aware of the means by which she had attained power, may be imagined. At first, however, they were not alarmed for their converts, or for the cause they were promoting. They knew, indeed, that the Queen was a besotted devotee of idolatry, and that priests and sorcerers and diviners would have her patronage and favour; nor were they unaware of the fact that the men whose bloodstained hands had lifted her to the throne, and who would support her there, were as bigoted as she. Still they hoped for the best, and laboured on; and as, for some time after Radama's death, their work was not impeded, they trusted that all would continue to go on well. Indeed, during the early part of her reign, she assisted in the erection of an additional place of worship in the capital, and did not interfere with the administration of Christian ordinances. Nevertheless, the Missionaries knew that the will of such a woman was a false and precarious ground of confidence. They therefore laboured more abundantly than before in teaching, preaching, translating, and printing, that, should their worst fears be realised, the fruit of their toil might not only, with God's blessing, abound, but abide. It is a cause for wonder and thankfulness, that these devoted labourers effected so much in the way of translations, during the brief and broken intervals they could abstract from more active occupations. Now it was that, in addition to a version of the Scriptures, they compiled two dictionaries, a grammar, and numerous school and other works of permanent value to the people. And no doubt but that He who sees the end from the beginning, put this purpose into their hearts, and gave them a more than ordinary measure of strength and skill for its efficient accomplishment; for seldom have labours such as theirs proved more necessary, or more productive of beneficial results.

In order to allay the fears of the friends of social progress and Christianity, Ranavalona, shortly after being proclaimed Queen, sent to inform the Missionaries that it was her purpose to tread in the footsteps of Radama; and not long after this, in a more public form, she solemnly engaged to carry out his plans for the education and improvement of the people. But while thus acting, her desire to sustain the reputation of the idols, to perpetuate the customs of her ancestors, and to destroy the rapidly-extending influence of the Europeans, could not be disguised. There was, however, a formidable obstacle on the threshold of that course of repression and violence by which her reign was subsequently characterised. At that time, her chief nobles and advisers formed two opposing parties. One of these was headed by a young officer named Andriamihaja, a great favourite of the Queen, and a friend of the Missionaries : the other was led by two brothers—Rainiharo and Rainimaharo, the former being the guardian of one of the chief idols, and both of them determined enemies to the Christians. For two years, the party of Andriamihaja was strong enough to prevent the retrograde movement which his rivals and the Queen desired ; but at length the idolatrous party prevailed. While in a state of intoxication, they procured from Ranavalona the death-warrant of Andriamihaja, who was immediately afterwards murdered in his own house.

Thus, one strong barrier was removed out of the path which the heathen party were anxious to take. Happily, however, the two years in which these factions had been contending for supremacy were well improved by the Missionaries, who laboured with increased energy and great success in preparing books and teaching the people. Contrary to their expectations, no material change appeared during this time in the conduct of the Queen; and even so late as the spring of 1831, she permitted her subjects to be baptized, and repeated her declaration that she would not "change the words of the King." But at the same time powerful influences, both from within and from without, were impelling her to do so. After the death of Andriamihaja, her only counsellors were the bitter foes of Christianity. This hostility, both on their part and on the part of other nobles, was continually kept alive by the fact, which was obvious both to themselves and to others, that, while they and their countrymen who followed the customs of their ancestors were not making the attainments in knowledge which Radama had recommended, those who professed Christianity, and attended the chapels and schools—many of them slaves—were becoming intelligent and upright. This humiliating contrast chafed and irritated the pagan party, and filled them with envy and wrath.

It was not long, however, before premonitory symptoms of approaching evil appeared. One of the first of these was an intimation to some Christian officers of the Government who were about to join the Church in the capital, that their so doing would be displeasing to their royal mistress. This was soon followed by a proclamation, prohibiting the soldiers, and those whom the Government had placed in the schools, from being baptized, or receiving the Lord's Supper. By the close of the same year (1831) a similar prohibition was extended to the people at large. Happily, no restrictions had as yet been put upon the liberty of the Missionaries to preach or print. In these departments, therefore, they continued to labour, if possible, more assiduously than ever. During the same anxious period God "gave testimony to the word of His grace." Not only were the congregations large, but a spirit of thoughtfulness and devotion appeared to pervade them; while cases of conversion, some of them remarkable, proved that He was in their midst. The Missionaries were also greatly cheered by the constancy of their converts in life and death. "I am going to Jesus. He calls me. I do not fear!" were the dying words of one of them; "simple words," as a Missionary wrote, which "presented as strong a contrast as human language can admit to the common feeling of the people. Those who have seen the strongest men in Madagascar die, know how, when stretched on a death-bed, they will exclaim in the anguish of despair, while the big tears trickle down their cheeks, 'I die! I die! I die! O father, O mother, I die!'" The readers, too, had multiplied by thousands, and the press had now sent forth the New Testament, and was scattering Christian books broadcast over the land. But, as it was obvious that the schools were only tolerated because some useful arts were taught in them, the Missionaries were not surprised when at length the jealousy of the Queen and the nobles was expressed in an order that no slave was any longer to attend them.

About the same time, the Rev. D. Griffiths was commanded to leave the country. One reason assigned for this order was that the term of five years, to which, in the first instance, Radama had restricted the term of residence to foreigners, had expired; but this was accompanied by the following message:—" You, Mr. Griffiths," said the Tsitialainga,* "are guilty of attempting to transport beyond sea some of her majesty's subjects. In proof of this, here is your blanket, which you gave to those people; here is your lanthorn, which you also gave them; and here is a letter of yours, which you also gave them to take with them. Now, if you had been a native of this land, the Queen would at once have put you to death; but as you are a foreigner, and as you in former times did much in the country, the Queen spares your life; but her sentence is, that you forthwith leave Antananarivo, and get beyond the sea." The execution of this sentence was afterwards suspended for a year; but then Mr. Griffiths, and soon afterwards the Rev. T. Atkinson, who had been but twelve months in the country, and Mr. Cannan, one of the Missionary artisans, were compelled to leave. Thus new links were being added to the iron chain of despotic restrictions which the Missionaries saw was gradually contracting the already too narrow sphere of their operations. Still, the process was slow, and even up to the beginning of the year 1835, there had been no interruption of public worship. At no previous period had the sanctuaries been so crowded, while there were few families, from those

---

* The meaning of this word is "Hater of Lies." It is the designation given to a large spear, highly ornamented with silver, with the Queen's name engraved upon it. The bearer or bearers of this symbol of office are known by the same term.

most nearly related to the Queen down to the households of the slaves, in which disciples of the Saviour could not be found. And it is most instructive and interesting to observe how by these and other circumstances the great Lord was providing for the maintenance and furtherance of His own cause, and at the same time was preparing His servants for the period, then so near, when, separated from those beloved and trusted guides who until now had been at hand to counsel, cheer, and help them, they would be thrown entirely upon Himself and upon their own resources. Without pressure from the Missionaries, and by a common impulse upon many minds, gifted and godly natives were now raised up to teach and preach Christ to their countrymen. He who said, "Separate me Barnabas and Saul for the work whereunto I have called them," had evidently given to these good men His own high authority to perform ministerial functions, together with some of the rarest and richest qualifications for the work. This strongly impressed the Missionaries themselves, two of whom thus wrote to the Directors in 1834. "God appears to manifest His purposes of mercy towards His people in raising up an agency of His own among themselves to carry on His own work. He is preparing His own instruments, giving them zeal and knowledge, imbuing them with love to the truth, and thus supplying the exigencies of His cause, and compensating for our lack of service."

At last the crisis came. No very powerful incitement was required to transform the latent hatred of the sovereign and her councillors into active hostility against the Christians. But this was now furnished. One Sabbath in February, as she was carried in her state palanquin through the city, Ranavalona passed a chapel while the congregation was singing, and immediately remarked to her attendants, "They will not stop till some of them lose their heads."

Soon after this she was told that many of the Christians, and amongst them a near connection of one of her chief ministers, had spoken disrespectfully of the idols. Imperfect or distorted reports of passages of sermons also reached the Queen's ear. These excited her. But she was chiefly exasperated by the doctrines of future retribution, and the general resurrection. "I myself," she exclaimed, "never heard such things as these, and if they had been true, I must have heard of them." About the same time, another incident came to her knowledge, which fanned the flame of her anger. A young man who during his residence in the capital had become a Christian, while visiting some friends in a village where an idol was kept, ventured rather freely to express his surprise that any person could be so ignorant as to trust a useless log of wood; an offence which was aggravated by the fact that he would not swear, nor work on the Sabbath, and that at night he drew the people to meet with him for prayer. These crimes were charged before the judge, and by him were reported to the Queen. That the guilt or innocence of the accused might appear, he was required to drink the tangena—the poison-water ordeal. The Christians trembled for their friend, but they also prayed, and God heard them. To express their joy at his deliverance, many residing in the capital imprudently marched in procession through the streets. This was reported to the Queen, and increased her anger. Seeing whither the stormy passions of the Queen were driving her, some of her nobles courageously pointed out the loss the kingdom would sustain by the destruction of her most enlightened and trustworthy subjects. She thanked them for their counsels, and it was hoped would have been swayed by them. Just afterwards, however, a chief of rank and influence having obtained admission to her presence thus addressed her: "I am come to ask your Majesty for a spear—a bright and sharp spear —grant my request." Being asked for what purpose he wanted the weapon, his answer was, that the idols—the guardians of the land—were dishonoured; that the hearts of the people were turned from the customs of their ancestors; that by their teaching and their books the Missionaries had drawn away many nobles and officers of the army, as well as people of the inferior orders; and that ruin would come upon the land unless these evils were speedily stopped; and "as," he added, "such will be the issue of the teaching of the foreigners, and as I do not wish to see that calamity come upon my country, I ask for a spear, to pierce my heart before the evil day comes." This appeal produced its designed effect. Greatly moved with grief and rage, the Queen first wept, then sat in silence for about half an hour, and at length solemnly declared that she would put an end to Christianity, if it cost the life of every Christian in her land. Her councillors and attendants fully apprehended the fearful import of her tearful silence and terrible threat. And they were the meet precursors of that outburst of vengeance which so soon, and for so long a period, desolated Madagascar. The following fortnight was strongly marked by evil omens. During that time profound silence prevailed within the palace. Music, dancing, and all other amusements were intermitted. The court appeared as if mourning over some dreadful disaster or death; and as the intelligence spread amongst the people, it filled a multitude of hearts with faintness and fear.

No time was lost in carrying out the royal threatening. Only a few days after its utterance, as the Missionaries were proceeding to their Thursday evening service, they received a summons to hear that message from the Queen which put a final stop to all their public labours.

On the 1st of March the people were convened for a kabary, or public assembly, to hear the royal prohibition of Christianity, and a command that all Christians should confess their crime within a month,* or suffer death. The day of trial and the reign of terror had now commenced. The profession of Christianity had become a capital crime in Madagascar.

During the following week, multitudes acknowledged that they had read Christian books, and attended Christian worship; and submitted themselves to the royal

* By a subsequent order restricted to a week.

pleasure. But there were others who disregarded the Queen's commands; and this they did, well knowing the consequences of refusal, but resolved to suffer rather than sin. That they might be able to act thus, prayer was made unto God, and never with more freedom or fervour than during that anxious week.

Let us in thought visit one or two of the hallowed spots where the Christians now met to commune with each other and with their common Lord. It is midnight. The darkness and silence are unbroken. No voice nor footstep is heard in the streets of the capital. But here and there, individuals might have been discerned silently stealing along under the deep shadows of the houses. All these are bending their steps towards one point—the house of prayer. Let us follow them, as they enter the place where God had often met and blessed them. A smile of loving recognition glances from face to face, tempered with a shade of sadness and anxiety. They join in prayer; but in the midst of their devotions a stranger enters. He is an officer of high rank in the army—an honourable and friendly man, but not hitherto known as a Christian. Filled with surprise, not unmixed with apprehension, the brethren suspend the service, and wait in silence for an explanation. This is frankly given. The officer declared himself to be one of their number, and added that he had been constrained to join them in this the hour of their weakness and peril, because he abhorred the injustice with which they had been treated by the Queen, and the cowardice with which the half-hearted had quailed before her uplifted arm. That was a memorable night in the history and experience of the Christians. He who thus, when others shrunk away, came bravely forth to share their perils, not fearing the wrath of the Queen, proved subsequently one of their wisest counsellors and best protectors. Soon, too, his wife followed his example, and, with her husband, succoured very many. Such an accession to their number at such a season was singularly calculated to confirm the faith and revive the courage of the little flock, and to enable them calmly to await the outburst of the lowering tempest. But this was not all. These meetings proved, in an unusual degree, "times of refreshing from the presence of the Lord," and of gracious preparation for the fiery trial which was to try them. Long were the midnight hours of that memorable week remembered as amongst the brightest and most blessed of their history:—hours, the sweet influence of which proved in after-days a solace and a support, when, separated from one another, these brethren beloved were working in chains, or concealed in forests, or immured in prisons, or anticipating a martyr's death.

But let us now enter another house in the capital during the same days of dark expectation. Again it is night. A few women are gathered within that dwelling. Their countenances betoken an anxiety which too well agrees with their communications. They are conversing about the edict of the Queen, and the punishments denounced against those who disregard it. Sad and disheartened, just as they are expressing to one another a fear lest their faith should fail in the hour of trial, an unexpected visitor enters. He was no stranger, but a Christian friend from a distant district; and soon it appeared that he had come there with a message from God. Delighted to see him, and assured of his sympathy, the women disclosed their depression and dread. "Have you read God's Word to-day?" he inquired. They told him that, in consequence of the confusion, they had been unable to do so. "Have you, then," he continued, "wrestled with God in prayer?" They replied that they had tried to give themselves up to Him, but that they had been overcome by terror. "I wonder not at this," said the friend; "let us read the 46th Psalm." With much feeling and solemnity, he then proceeded: "God is our refuge and strength; a very present help in trouble. Therefore will not we fear," &c. After this they kneeled down together, this Christian man conducting their devotions. The sacred exercise brought with it new life and strength. From that hour, the trembling women became courageous; and long afterwards some of them declared that, whenever anxious thoughts threw a gloomy shadow upon their path, they scattered them by again reading the 46th Psalm.

The dark and portentous days of that dreadful week were now numbered; and another kabary was summoned, at which it was known that the sentences of the Christians would be pronounced. A large multitude was collected when the judges appeared, holding in their hands the Queen's decree. It began by assuring the Christians that their crimes deserved death, and that, had not the people of the province (Imerina) interceded for them, she would have driven them all down the river and over the cataract. Punishments would therefore be awarded which were far lighter than their deserts. The sentences were then read, which deprived four hundred officers and nobles of their honours, and levied fines upon the remainder to the number of about two thousand.

This award was followed by another royal mandate, which required all books to be delivered up to the officers, and threatened death against any who kept back, or hid even a single leaf.* But like other persecutors, this besotted woman in her blind fury would fain have rivetted her fetters upon the souls of her subjects. With a mad infatuation which provokes a smile, she claimed the right and the power to restrain the free exercise of the mind, and commanded her subjects never again even to think upon the Christian lessons they had learned, but to blot them from their memories for ever!

Amongst the important services which the Missionaries rendered to the Christian cause in the interval between the suppression of public worship and their departure from the

* Some of the reasons assigned for the condemnation of certain books were strange and ludicrous. When they were collected, the Queen appointed four of her officers to examine them. They began with the Bible, because it was the largest book. In the first verse of the Book of Genesis they found nothing to which they could take exception, but in the second came the word "darkness." That was sufficient ground for condemnation, because the Queen did not like darkness. Sentence against the Bible was therefore pronounced without further examination. Other books were, in like manner, made offenders for a word.

capital, there was one which, in the times of trial now impending, proved inestimable. This was the translation of the " Pilgrim's Progress." Eight copies were transcribed by the Christians for their use in common. And well did they study and wisely apply the teachings of that noble allegory. Often amidst their wanderings, did its scenery and sayings recur to their memories, and cheer their hearts. Next to the Bible, this was the book which the persecuted Malagasy most prized. One copy, we are told, was found upon a Christian when he was apprehended, and was carefully scrutinised by the Queen's officers; but after vainly attempting to penetrate its mysteries and discover its meaning, they abandoned the task in despair.

But valuable as this service was to the Christians, there was another rendered by the Missionaries at this time, of far higher importance—the completion of the printing of the Scriptures in the Malagasy language. The native printers, indeed, had been forbidden to aid in this or any other work connected with the Mission, but, with strange inconsistency, the Queen permitted Mr. Baker and other Missionaries to remain in the capital, though she must have known that they were preparing and printing prohibited books. This was a happy oversight, and one which went far to neutralize her subsequent endeavours to uproot Christianity from the land.

The Christians also partook of the Lord's Supper together in secret, and not a few even during this time of terror were added to their number. Some, fearing that after their teachers had left it would be impossible to procure the Word of God, travelled as far as a hundred miles for a copy. One poor man, though he had been confined to his house by illness for many months, nevertheless walked sixty miles to make this much-coveted treasure his own, and when the Missionary placed a Bible in his hand, his countenance became radiant with joy. He pressed the sacred volume to his bosom, and said, "This contains the words of eternal life; it is my life, and I will take as much care of it as of my own life!" And he did as he had said; though driven from his home, and compelled to hide himself in the forests, he proved faithful unto death.

At length, in 1835, it became but too obvious that the labours of the Missionaries in Madagascar must terminate. Most of them, therefore, left the capital during that year. Messrs. Johns and Baker still lingered through a season of suspense, anxiety, and pain, until the following summer, but then, with heavy hearts, they turned from the scenes of labour which had yielded much and promised more, and with tearful eyes and sinking hearts said farewell to many whom they were forced to leave as sheep in the midst of wolves, whose faces they would see no more. Well aware of the existence of a number of the much-hated sect, in spite of her edicts and punishments, and yet unable to convict them, the rage of the Queen continued to increase. At the same time, the Christians were becoming better known to one another, and all of them did what they could to encourage themselves and each other in the Lord. For this purpose they held many secret meetings, sometimes in solitary houses or other secluded spots, but more frequently upon the summits of mountains, from whence they could observe the approach of strangers, and where they could not only read God's Word and pray, but engage with loud voice in the, to them, sweet and sacred exercise of vocal praise. And as they now possessed seventy copies of the entire Scriptures, with a still larger number of New Testaments, Psalms, and Christian books, which were always carefully concealed and often buried in the ground until wanted for use, they had in their hands means of instruction and consolation which they knew well how to employ.

Amongst the most devoted of this Christian band was the well-remembered Rafaravavy. Prior to her conversion she had been a zealous upholder of idolatry, but from the time her heart was given to the Saviour, she consecrated her property, influence and energy to His service. At length she was accused by three of her slaves of attending religious meetings. On hearing of this accusation, the Queen exclaimed, "Is it possible that there is one so daring as to defy me! Go and put her at once to death." But the intercession of friends and the former services of her father induced the Queen to commute the sentence into a heavy fine.

The calm, firm, heroic, and yet gentle bearing of this noble Christian lady, both at this trying period and subsequently while pursuing the path of duty, surrounded by perils, and in the near view of martyrdom, has rarely been equalled, and never surpassed. "I shall never forget," wrote Mr. Johns, "the serenity and composure she displayed while she related to me the consolations she enjoyed in pleading the promises and in drawing near to God in prayer." It is not surprising that the spirit and conduct of such a woman should greatly comfort and confirm her fellow-sufferers.

For some months after the departure of the Missionaries, the Christians enjoyed comparative peace. This appears to have arisen from a persuasion on the part of their oppressors that, when thus left to themselves, they would soon return to their former practices. Instead of this, however, all the letters forwarded to their exiled friends indicated that the joy of the Lord was their strength, that some who had drawn back were restored, and that their number was on the increase. Thus even their loss proved to them gain. "The Queen does not know," they write, "that the best teacher of all is still here with us, the Holy Spirit." One valued and honoured man was taken from them; but his holy life, closed by a truly Christian death, tended to strengthen the faith and animate the hopes of the survivors. They designate him "a beloved brother," and speak of the great delight and benefit which they derived from his society. He was a young man, and remarkable for the depth and tenderness of his love to the Divine Redeemer. Both Missionaries and Christians were struck with the circumstance, that, whenever he named the name of Jesus, it brought tears to his eyes; and when he was asked the reason of this, his simple answer was, "How can I do otherwise than feel, while I mention the name of that beloved Saviour, who suffered and died on the cross for me?" As the hour of his departure drew near, a

Christian brother inquired whether he had any fear of death. "Why should I fear to die," he exclaimed, "while Jesus is my friend? He hath loved me with an everlasting love, and I love Him because He hath first loved me. I am persuaded that He will not leave me now, for I am full of joy at the thought of leaving this sinful world to be for ever with my Saviour." "We trust," write some of the Christians to Mr. Johns, "his death will stimulate us to labour in the work of the Lord while it is day."

But the diligence with which the Christians had improved this brief remission of severe punishment, and the consequent increase both of their numbers and influence in the capital and country, had been so contrary to the calculations of their enemies, that the Queen and her councillors resolved to adopt more severe measures for their repression.*

* It is impossible to determine the exact number of those who, when the Missionaries left the country, were regarded by them and each other as enlightened and spiritual Christians. It has been generally supposed that these were about 200, and there is reason for supposing that this estimate, to say the least, is not too high. We find, at the close of 1831, that there were 87 in Church fellowship in the two churches at the capital. But the Missionaries write that there were also as "many who evince a concern for their souls," that "the work of the Spirit appears to be going on," that the number of inquirers is increasing, and that "those who have been savingly converted are zealous in spreading the knowledge of the Gospel, and in bringing their friends and relatives to a participation of that salvation which it is their own happiness to enjoy." Two years after this, they state that their congregations are good, and that their appearance indicated a serious and devout regard to the Word of God. We are told, also, in the following year, of the erection of a small chapel, and "a delightful spirit of inquiry awakened in a district

This change first appeared in an accusation which was lodged against fourteen Christians, ten of whom were a fortnight afterwards apprehended and condemned to perpetual slavery. One of these was Rafaravavy; but, specially to show the Queen's displeasure, the rabble received the royal permission to raze her house and seize her property. This having been done, she was chained, imprisoned, and condemned to be executed on the following morning. But during the previous night, a fire broke out in the capital, which aroused the superstitious fears of Ranavalona, and saved Rafaravavy's life. Thus the honour of being the proto-martyr of Madagascar was reserved for another.

Amongst the ten who were now imprisoned, was a young woman named Rasalama. While under confinement, she was overheard to express her astonishment that she and her Christian friends should receive such treatment. "Men," she exclaimed, "that have neither excited rebellion, nor stolen the property of any, nor spoken ill of any —yet all their property is confiscated, and they themselves reduced to perpetual slavery. I would advise the persecutors to think a little of what they are doing, lest they bring on themselves the wrath of God;" and then, with much warmth, she added, "When the Tsitialaingia came to my house, I was not afraid, but rather rejoiced that

---

sixty miles from the capital," and of another chapel 120 miles distant. These, and other manifestations of spiritual life and progress appear to justify the belief that not less than 200, and probably more than that number of earnest Christians, existed in the country when the Missionaries were compelled to leave it.

I was counted worthy to suffer affliction for believing in Jesus." This utterance having been reported to the judges, she was ordered to be put into heavy irons and severely beaten; but throughout these sufferings, so long as she had strength, she sought comfort in singing her favourite hymns. Her firmness and fortitude confounded her persecutors, and astonished the people; and the only solution of the mystery which they could imagine, was that she was under the influence of some very powerful charm. There were those, however, who looked at her calm countenance, and listened to her triumphal words with far different thoughts and feelings.

During the afternoon preceding the day of her execution, the ordinary chains she wore were exchanged for others, consisting of rings and bars fastened around her hands, feet, knees, and neck, which were then drawn together, and thus the whole body was forced into a position which caused great agony. This was its intended effect. It was done, not for security, but simply for punishment. Joyful, therefore, was the patient sufferer as the time drew on when death would rescue her from the tyrant's power. And seldom has the dawning of day after a night of dreams, and restlessness and terror proved more reviving to the sick and the sorrowful than when it came to Rasalama. To her it was the hour of release and redemption. As she was led away she continued to sing, and thus set an example to be followed afterwards by many who were called to tread the same pathway to death and heaven. When passing the sanctuary in which she had been accustomed to worship, she exclaimed, "There I heard the words of the Saviour!" Though many sympathised with Rasalama, and earnest prayers were offered on her behalf by Christian friends, they knew that, by identifying themselves with her, the little aid they could render her would be at the peril of their own lives. But there was one whom danger did not deter. He was a young man, who, as it appeared, possessed her spirit, and was prepared to follow in her footsteps; his name was Rafaralahy. Deaf to prudential considerations, and fearless of consequences, he pressed through the guard of soldiers by whom Rasalama was surrounded, and, walking as near to her side as he could, he said to her, "My sister, I will not leave you till the end!" At length the gloomy procession reached the spot where this Christian woman was to suffer. The name of it is Ambohipotsy. It forms the southern extremity of the crest of the hill upon which the city stands.

When Mr. Ellis and the Bishop of Mauritius lately visited it, they saw there the remains of the broken cross, upon which many had hung in anguish, and in a ditch just by were strewed the bleached bones of Christian martyrs—sad memorials of dark days and darker deeds, now soon to be buried, though not forgotten, beneath a sanctuary which, while it enshrines the memory of many heroic sufferers, will honour the Saviour whom they loved, and for whom they died, and extend the knowledge of His salvation. "The subdued and yet eager manner," writes the Bishop, " in which the native Christians described what had happened, was quite exciting to witness. It made old stories of martyrdom appear quite recent and fresh. From the parts interpreted and explained to me, I gathered the following facts. That the Christians went to their death with cheerful countenance, singing hymns as long as they were able to do so. Straw was stuffed into their mouths by their persecutors to stop them, but until violently hindered, they sang loudly the praises of God. Some of the heathens, who were particularly desirous of seeing how they behaved when the last hour of suffering came, confessed afterwards that nothing so impressed them as the courageous demeanour and glad singing of those who were being led to death. A large crowd seems to have followed on the occasion to which our friends referred, with shouting and imprecations against the Christians. The victims were taken into the ditch, and made to bend forward, and then two spears were struck into their bodies, one on each side of the backbone; and when they fell prostrate with their wounds, their heads were cut off, and placed in rows along the edge of the ditch. The heads of five members of one family were placed thus in a row on one occasion, and thirteen others behind them, and were left a long time there, till removed secretly, as I understood, by their friends. The whole scene," adds the Bishop, " the description, the mournful tone of voice, the affectionate earnestness of manner of those who told us, some of whom had been for years exposed to the most imminent danger themselves, all produced a most solemn effect on the mind."

A member of the British embassy, who subsequently

visited this spot, thus writes: "To an English mind it was scarcely possible in this age of the world to realize the hard, dry fact that the stump of wood was the foot of a cross on which our Christian brethren had been crucified, and that the bleached and lifeless bones in the ditch were those of men and women who had died but a few years ago for the name of the Saviour; that on the spot where we now stood, and had surveyed one of the noblest panoramas in nature, had knelt these martyrs 'of whom the world was not worthy,' while a spear was being driven through either loin, inflicting mortal wounds that did not kill at once, but made the wretched sufferers roll in torture into the ditch below with the spears still fixed in their bodies; while even the nearest and dearest relative dared not soothe one dying struggle, or evince by a look of sympathy a doubt of the justice of the punishment."

This, then, was the place to which Rasalama was conducted. But the scene did not disturb the deep calm of her spirit. Though reviled by the heathen, she rested upon the Saviour, and reviled not again. The only request she made to her executioners was for a brief interval, that she might pray. This was granted, and she kneeled down upon the rocky ground. Some said, "Where is the God she prays to, that He does not save her now?" Others looked on with pity. But she, regardless of all around, held communion with the Divine Saviour; and while thus commending her spirit into His hands, the executioners from behind buried their spears in her body. So calm, so firm was this noble sufferer, that even the hard men who took her life were constrained to say, "There is some charm in the religion of the white people, which takes away the fear of death;" while that courageous friend who had accompanied her to the last exclaimed, as he turned from a spectacle at once so sorrowful and so sublime, "If I might die so tranquil and happy a death, I would not be unwilling to die for the Saviour too."

We cannot give a circumstantial history of the other Christians who were apprehended with Rasalama. They all were condemned to hard bondage; but five of them had the great comfort of working together. Their master, indeed, Rainiharo, was their cruel persecutor, and they had much to endure—toiling hard during the day, and heavily ironed at night. But still they could speak often one to another; and Paul, who though weak in body was strong in spirit, contributed not a little to the comfort of his companions in tribulation by repeating the 46th Psalm, and other passages of the Scriptures with which his memory was stored. He possessed also copies of the Psalter, and a Christian Catechism, while another had preserved in secret a tract on the Resurrection; and when all was dark and still, these precious treasures were drawn out from their hiding-places, and read aloud. This exercise and prayer lightened their heavy load, and brought them much peace.

Two others, David and Simeon, were assigned to a wretch, distinguished amongst his fellows for his cruel disposition—a bad pre-eminence, with which his treatment of these good men but too well accorded. After three months, they were transferred to this tyrant's son, but not until they had drank the tangena, to show whether they possessed the power of witchcraft. This dangerous ordeal had nearly cost David's life, but God delivered him.

Amongst the nine who had been condemned, Rafaravavy appears to have been the greatest sufferer. For a long period she was loaded with heavy chains, and daily expected to be led forth to the place of execution; but while in prison, even at the risk of their own liberty, she was visited by loving Christian friends, who ministered to her comfort by their counsels and their prayers. Hiding within the folds of their lambas some portions of the Scriptures, they would steal away to the prison, and there, in a suppressed and muffled voice, pour into her ear the sacred and soul-reviving words of life and peace. Such conduct was characteristic of the Christianity of these true-hearted followers of the Saviour. Theirs was the "perfect love" to Him and to His which "casteth out fear." While as cautious as circumstances permitted, they were yet "strong and of good courage;" feelings which were doubtless confirmed by the conviction that their beloved and honoured friend would soon need their kind offices no more. But, contrary to expectation, her life was spared, and at the end of five months she was sold into perpetual slavery. Providentially, however, and without a suspicion of the kind on the part of her persecutors, her master was a humane man, and her mistress proved to be a relative. Some liberty was therefore allowed to her, which she gladly and assiduously improved. Hence, as soon as her daily task was done, she hastened to the dwellings of her fellow-Christians. And amongst those with whom it was her delight to meet for prayer and praise, was Rafaralahy, the companion and comforter of Rasalama when on her way to the scene of her martyrdom. He lived about two miles from the capital, and made it the study of his life to minister to the wants and promote the welfare of his Christian brethren. He had been one of Rafaralahy's most constant visitors during her imprisonment. His property and his time were devoted to the one great object of doing good. With this intent he had built a house in a retired spot near his own dwelling, specially that the brethren might meet there for worship; and here they were often found in fellowship with each other and the Lord. At the same time he laboured to draw others into the way of life, amongst whom there were three lepers, for whose interests, temporal as well as spiritual, he was peculiarly solicitous. These poor outcasts from society were shunned and loathed by all except this Christian man. But in him they found a true friend. He sheltered them, fed them, and taught them to read that blessed book which had brought peace to his own spirit. And "with such sacrifices God was well pleased." One of the lepers preceded his benefactor to heaven, and there is reason to hope that the others soon followed him thither.

At length, a false professor who owed Rafaralahy money and much beside, hoping to release himself from his obligation, accused his benefactor of holding religious meetings in his house. He was in consequence seized, loaded with chains, and committed to prison. But he "suffered as a Christian," and experienced that Divine support which enabled him, without fear or faltering, to be "faithful unto death." During the brief period of his confinement, severe measures were employed to extort from him the names of his Christian associates; but his unvarying answer to every persuasive and every threat, was, "Here am I, let the Queen do what she pleases with me; I have done it, but I will not accuse my friends." After an imprisonment of two or three days, the minister of death entered his prison; and as soon as he inquired, "Which is Rafaralahy?" the brave man promptly answered, "I am, sir!" His irons were then struck off, and he was led forth to the place of execution. Doubtless, as he walked towards it, he remembered Rasalama, who had preceded him there, and could not have forgotten the strong sympathy and Christian love which then constrained him to draw near to her, and to whisper in her ear, "My sister, I will not leave you till the end!" Though it does not appear that he sang, as she did, on his way to the fatal spot, we are told that he spoke to those around him of the Saviour, and of the sacred joy he felt in the near prospect of beholding Him. On reaching Ambohipotsy, following the example of Rasalama, he requested a brief space for prayer, and kneeling down upon the ground consecrated by her blood and strewed with her unburied bones, he looked up stedfastly into heaven, prayed for his country and his brethren, and having committed his soul to his Divine Redeemer, he arose from the ground, "ready to be offered." When the executioners were about to throw him down, he assured them that force was unnecessary, as he was quite willing to die. He then laid himself upon the ground, and in a few moments he had entered into the joy of the Lord. The calmness and firmness with which he met death made, we are told, "a deep impression upon the minds of his persecutors."

Immediately after his execution, the wife of Rafaralahy and another female were seized and subjected to torture, to induce them to inculpate his associates. In a moment of weakness, produced by suffering and fear, they made the disclosure. Friends, however, were within hearing, who caught the names of some of the accused, and amongst these that of Rafaravavy. No time was lost in warning her of her danger. She was sitting with three of her fellow-Christians conversing upon the subjects in which they were most deeply interested, when a servant hastily entered the room and put a note into her hand. It conveyed the intelligence that Rafaralahy had been executed, and that unless she and others instantly fled, nothing could save them. After a brief conference, the three women proceeded towards the city, and having reached the outskirts, almost under the shadow of the dreadful Ambohipotsy, they kneeled down, commended each other to God, and then separated, to meet no more on earth. Rafaravavy, to whom escape now seemed impossible, but for whom death had no terrors, ventured to call at her master's house, almost expecting to find officers awaiting her there. After this, she hastened to confer with David, Simeon, and others of the accused, as to the course they should pursue. This appeared very clear to all of them. They remembered the Saviour's injunction to the persecuted, and resolved upon immediate flight. As Simeon and David, who were slaves of Rainiharo, held money and cloth belonging to their master, their first concern was to draw up an accurate account of all sales and receipts, and to leave this paper with the balance of money due to him, and what remained of his unsold property. This proceeding was something new on the part of slaves; and it was not surprising, when such evidence of integrity came into his hands, that the oppressor of the Christians was astonished, and exclaimed, " These would make excellent servants, if they would but leave off their religion." It was midnight before their preparations were completed, and time that the fugitives should leave the city. But this was not possible to Simeon, in consequence of the illness of his wife; nor to Paul and others, who lived too far off to be apprised in time of the movements of their brethren. Hence only five could avail themselves of the opportunity—Joseph, David and his wife, Andrianimanana, and Rafaravavy.

And it was well for them that they acted with promptitude, for, on the following morning, messengers with a death-warrant from the Queen hastened to every place where it was thought probable that Rafaravavy might be concealed.

A detailed history of these Christian fugitives has been already furnished in the deeply interesting narrative of Freeman and Johns. We shall, therefore, only briefly recall such of their many dangers and deliverances as most strikingly indicate the protecting care of Providence, and the strength of Christian principle, manifested not only by themselves, but by others. With this view we should remember that all who sheltered, fed, or in any way assisted the Christians, exposed themselves to the same condemnation. Yet notwithstanding, wherever brethren dwelt, there was a home for the wandering; and thither they hasted, with a full assurance of a welcome and a hiding-place. Indeed, all who had a common faith seemed to be inspired by the strongest desire to succour each other, at whatever risk to themselves.

Fifty miles from the capital, at a place named Itanimanina, lived a Christian and his wife. To their abode the five fugitives first directed their steps. Here they met with the reception they expected; and, though exhausted with journeying and loss of sleep, the night after their arrival was mostly spent in prayer and praise, in the recital of recent events, and in the expression of anxiety for Paul, and others, whom they had left behind. This anxiety, and the impossibility of concealing five strangers in one house, induced two of them to proceed to Paul's village, although the distance was thirty-five miles. But, on reaching it, they were distressed to learn that their friend was a prisoner. As, therefore, they were unable to help him they returned to Itanimanina.

About this time, a message came to them from another Christian in the same district to this effect: " Let all the Christians who are compelled to run away for their lives, come to me. I will take care of them. As long as I am safe, they are safe; and as long as I have food, they shall share it." But just then this loving invitation was not accepted, Joseph and David having previously arranged to seek a refuge in the forest far on the other side of the capital. Thither, through dangers and with much difficulty, they at length found their way; and here Simeon, who until now had been concealed over an oven in a friend's house at the capital, soon afterwards joined them. Only one man,—strange to say, a servant of the Government,— knew their hiding-place, and he would not reveal it even to his nearest connections. As the forest furnished fuel only and not food, this noble specimen of a friend and a brother, though naturally a timid man, ventured his own life to save theirs; and as often as he could leave his home, he walked from fifty to sixty miles, carrying a heavy burden of rice over rugged roads and through the tangled forest, to their hiding-place. Thus, by self-sacrificing love and labour, they were sustained nearly six months, when it became necessary for them to seek another refuge.

Meanwhile, Rafaravavy remained at Itanimanina. But soldiers were now upon her track; great caution and vigilance were therefore essential. Every morning, ere the day dawned, she and Sarah crept to a lonely mountain, where they hid themselves amidst the craggy rocks; and at night they returned to their friend's house. But soon even this care was no longer to avail her. Her place of concealment had become known to Rainiharo, who at once despatched soldiers to apprehend her. Apprised of her daily hiding-place, before they entered the village they searched the mountain; but, contrary to her custom, the cold had induced Rafaravavy that day to remain at home. Having failed to find her amidst the rocks, the soldiers hastened towards the house unperceived, had come within sight of it, and were approaching the door. There was now but a step between her and death; yet by one of those simple and, as some might deem it, insignificant agencies which Divine Providence often employs, the Christian woman was rescued from her imminent danger. Though the soldiers created no alarm within the house, their hasty movements frightened some crows that were near it; and fearing from their noise that the birds were stealing the rice which had been spread out to dry, Sarah ran out to drive the depredators away, when, to her surprise and alarm, she saw two soldiers approaching. In a low tone she warned her friend of the danger, and Rafaravavy had just time enough to creep under a bedstead in the next room, and to cover herself up with a mat, ere the men entered. Happily, they did not search the house, but, during their stay there of an hour, she heard all they said respecting her, and the orders which had been issued for her death. But calm in the midst of this peril, she comforted herself with the words, "Be not afraid of sudden fear, neither of the desolation of the wicked when it cometh, for the Lord shall be thy confidence, and shall keep thy foot from being taken." Often, in other days of danger, did she and her friends recall this remarkable deliverance, and strengthen themselves in the Lord. While the soldiers were in the house, Simeon, who until now had been concealed in the capital, arrived there, and but for Sarah's great presence of mind, would have been captured.

But it was now quite time for Rafaravavy and Sarah—together with their kind and most disinterested protectors,—who had cheerfully risked all, and were willing to lay down their own necks for the sake of their brethren—to seek a safer habitation. After hiding for a short time in the houses of friendly neighbours, they travelled during the night to a distant village, where they were sure to find Christian hospitality. Having been concealed here for a few days, they went some distance further. to the abode of a relative, but had scarcely reached it, when they heard that soldiers were searching the neighbourhood for some woman that had run away. They therefore returned to the place they had left the day before, but the first intelligence that greeted them was that a party of soldiers was then in the village in quest of them. The pious woman who warned them of the danger hid them for that night in a pit, from which dreary refuge she conducted them on the following morning to a plantation of her own. Here they remained for some days undiscovered, though they saw the men who were in pursuit of them pass near to their hiding-place.

There were now about a hundred soldiers prosecuting the search. It was therefore arranged that they should become two bands, but the "hair-breadth 'scapes" of both parties were still many and remarkable. Once, as Rafaravavy with her two companions reached the crest of a hill, a lad who preceded them saw a company of soldiers marching towards them. At once her companions ran; but as she was unable to follow them, she plunged into a bog that was at hand; and it was only by lying half buried in mud, with her head screened by rushes, that she eluded observation.

But the hearts and hopes of the wanderers were now set upon the house of another Christian friend, where they knew that a loving welcome awaited them. Under the shadow of night, and through a country infested with robbers, they pressed on towards the much longed-for resting-place. At length, wearied with the journey, they reached their destination. As soon as their friend saw them, he burst into tears; but they were tears of joy at their unhoped-for deliverance out of the power of the armed bands who were scouring that part of the country in search of them. Here again was another striking manifestation of Christian confidence and affection which it is refreshing to contemplate. The fugitives, though fully aware of the danger to which their presence under his roof would expose their friend, nevertheless went thither, assured that his love to them for Christ's sake was superior to danger and stronger than death; whilst he, deaf to the suggestions of expediency and to the pleadings of selfishness, was ready to risk all for the privilege of affording these persecuted ones the aid and comfort which his loving heart could prompt, or his liberal hand supply.

It was, however, not an easy thing to shield the stranger guests from observation. At first an attempt was made to dig a hiding-place for them under a part of the house; but, failing in this, their host fixed a tent in the centre of a plantation of which he was the proprietor, where the high grass, and a prohibition against trespassers, promised well for their safety. Here, for three months, they were supplied and guarded. But these were not months of mere solitary musings and silent devotions. In common with their friend, the Christians desired to spend the time for the profit of others as well as themselves; and this desire was fulfilled. Every Sabbath a band of brethren met together for worship. And some who were not believers were nevertheless intrusted with the strangers' secret, and admitted to their society. Thus nearly twenty, during their sojourn, learned to read, and several members of the good man's family became decided followers of the Saviour. How obviously in this instance did the kindness shown in the name of a disciple meet with its rich reward!

At length the soldiers, foiled in their search, returned to the capital, and the Christians could once more breathe freely. Just about this time a letter from a friend informed them that Mr. Johns had come to Tamatave to aid their escape. But they were now on the western side of Tananarivo, a long distance from the coast, which could only be reached by passing through the capital. Yet, though the danger of the journey was imminent, their desire of deliverance, and their trust in Him who had hitherto been their shield, decided them to make the attempt.

Disguised as the servant of Andrianilaina and his wife, Rafaravavy commenced the perilous enterprise, but as she was entering the capital she was recognised by a slave, who reported the discovery to her former master. Happily, he disregarded the girl's assertion, and took no measures to ascertain its truth. While in the capital, the house where she was hiding herself was searched by a party of men, and once more she experienced a marvellous escape.

Soon all the fugitives met in Antananarivo, and here they remained while two friends hastened down to Tamatave, to make arrangements with Mr. Johns for their escape. On their return the party, consisting of Rafaravavy, Sarah, David, Simeon and Joseph, with two friends who accompanied them as servants, commenced their perilous journey towards the coast, amidst the tears and prayers of their beloved brethren. For four days and nights after their departure they did not enter a house, and their fears kept them in a state of almost sleepless vigilance. But God's word, and passages from the "Pilgrim's Progress," which shadowed forth something of their own condition, brought them peace in the midst of trouble. As they had to pass through villages where Rafaravavy was known, and to shun the observation of many soldiers who were travelling the same road, the constant and severe strain upon their spirits and strength was most exhausting. Once and again they lost their way in the almost pathless forest; but they pressed on until they reached the river Mangoro, which swarms with crocodiles, and the only way to cross which was in a Government canoe. Happily, the boatman had no suspicions, and made no inquiry. At length, through difficulties and dangers which cannot here be detailed, their weary eyes were gladdened by the gleam of the sea. But now their food was exhausted, and the distance to Tamatave was still great. There, however, a kind and influential Christian friend, who held a high appointment under the Government, and who subsequently had to save his life by escaping to Mauritius, was expecting them, and as soon as he heard of their approach, he sent a canoe to convey them to a house which he had prepared for them in a situation where the danger of discovery was but slight. Who can describe the gratitude and joy with which, on entering this new abode, they united with their protector in reading the 16th chapter of the Gospel by John, and in pouring out the fulness of their hearts before God in prayer and praise!

Apprised of their approach, with the concurrence of their native friend, Mr. Johns returned to Mauritius to charter a vessel; and after a few days, disguised as sailors, they embarked for that island. While the ship was leaving the harbour of Tamatave the captain said to them, "That business is over; all is safe!" At this they burst into tears, and then asked permission to sing. "Let us now," they said, "like Abraham's servant, bless the Lord, for He has prospered our journey, and granted our request. Blessed be the God and Father of our Lord Jesus Christ, who has not left us to perish by the hand of the enemy. Our souls are escaped like a bird from the snare of the fowler." How they were received at Mauritius, at the Cape of Good Hope, and in England, need not here be told. Thankful and joyful as they were, however, in view of their own great deliverance, their hearts turned sorrowfully back towards Madagascar, as they thought of the dear friends they had left behind them there, and received the intelligence that an order had been issued by the Queen, that, wherever Christians were discovered, they should be tied by their hands and feet, that a pit should be dug upon the spot, and that, having been thrust into it head foremost, boiling water should be poured upon their bodies until they were dead. The bitterness of this sad news was rendered more intense by a letter from their fugitive brethren, in which they write, "We have heard of the orders of the Queen respecting us, and in what manner we are to be put to death. We still confide in the compassion of the Saviour; but we ask, 'Can you do anything to rescue us?' We think of the death awaiting us. The spirit is willing, but the flesh is weak."

Foiled in all her efforts to apprehend the Christians, and learning that Rafaravavy and others, for whom the soldiers had so long searched, had effected their escape, the fury of the Queen flamed forth more fiercely than before. It was enough now if any were merely suspected of being Christians, to bring them under the oppressor's rod. Three women dwelt in the capital who were supposed to be Christians, two of whom were the wives of Simeon and David, then safe in a Christian land. Without positive evidence of their Christianity, an official was ordered to apprehend them. Happily, when he reached the house where he expected to find them, one was absent, and another had fled on hearing his errand; but the rough man rudely seized the third woman, and while beating her, a copy of the Bible fell from her dress. This, of course, made her guilt manifest. She was in consequence cruelly scourged even to fainting, with a view to extort from her the names of her companions. But torture could not loose her tongue, or shake her constancy. She was therefore condemned to perpetual slavery, while her friends sought a refuge in the forest.

But all could not flee. One young woman remained whose eminent piety, while it secured for her the warm love of her Christian associates, called forth the bitter hatred of her own family, who were bigoted heathens. Her father's house was closed against her; she was scorned and repudiated by her husband, while all her other relatives sympathized with their anger and aversion. Having obtained her condemnation as a Christian, she was sentenced to unredeemable slavery. It might have been imagined that a doom so severe would have satisfied them; but it was not so. They thirsted and plotted for her life, and at last, by a subtle device, obtained a decree that she should drink the tangena. The poison-cup proved fatal. The wretched relatives had now satiated their vengeance, but they had added another to the honoured band of Madagascar martyrs. The name of this Christian sufferer was Ravahiny, and it will be remembered with love and honour when that of her wretched murderers have perished.

In the hope of rendering valuable aid to the Christian sufferers, in July, 1840, Mr. Johns, who had remained until this time at Mauritius, ventured to revisit the capital but on reaching it, he received the sad intelligence that fourteen Christians had been captured, and were then in chains awaiting their trial. Their history was soon learned. Nearly two years before, like so many of their brethren, they, with two others, making a party of sixteen, resolved, if possible, to flee from the tyranny of the Queen. With this view they set out towards Tamatave, and had, after long wandering, reached a village called Beforona, which was within three or four days' journey of the coast; but unhappily the suspicion of some officers who saw them there was awakened by their appearance, and by the circumstance that they travelled through bye-paths, and at night. They were, in consequence, taken into custody. After three days' examination, during which nothing of importance had been elicited, they resolved to acknowledge who they were. Accordingly, one of them stood forth and thus spoke: "Since you ask us again and again, we will tell you. We are not robbers, nor murderers. We are praying people; and if this make us guilty in the kingdom of the Queen, then, whatsoever she does, that we must submit to suffer." "Is this, then," inquired the officer, "your final answer, whether for life or for death?" "It is," they rejoined, "our final answer, whether for life or for death."

The captives were then bound, and marched off towards Antananarivo. Two of them, however, happily escaped during the night, but the remainder were brought to the capital. Though they well knew what awaited them, their faith triumphed over fear. Firm and calm throughout the examination to which they were separately subjected, they witnessed a good confession, and avowed their readiness to die for the name of the Lord Jesus.

This sad intelligence greatly distressed Mr. Johns, and the more so because he knew that no appeals to the justice or the mercy of the inexorable Queen would turn her from her purpose. His only refuge, and that of the Christians with whom he secretly conferred, was the Divine throne; and there they often met, and the burden of their prayers was that their brethren might not faint in the day of danger, or prove faithless in the prospect of death. And God gave them the desire of their hearts.

Early one morning, after he had been in the capital but a few days, Mr. Johns was startled by the firing of cannon. This was an unusual sound, and he well knew that it betokened something extraordinary; but what, he could not learn. At length the heavy tidings reached him and oppressed his heart, that nine of the fourteen Christians were that day to die. He knew them all, and loved them much. They had been amongst the first ripe fruit of missionary labour, and were deservedly honoured by their brethren. Amongst them was Paul and Joshua, with their wives, and the wife of David, who had escaped to England. But besides these, there was another who was greatly beloved, and whose name and memory are still fragrant in Madagascar. This was Ramanisa, who took the baptismal name of Josiah. Before the persecution, he had been a faithful preacher of the Gospel; and when trouble came, he was not only himself prepared to endure it, but was earnest and active in strengthening others. Despairing of the Christians' liberty, for which he longed, he resolved to accompany his brethren in their attempt to find a refuge and a resting-place beyond their native shores. And greatly did they value his presence; he was to them a guide and a pastor, ministering counsel and consolation when most needed, while they were lurking in caves, or travelling by night, or wandering in forest solitudes. In these dark days his cheering words and fervent prayers made them "strong in the Lord," and "joyful in tribulation." This good man was the author of a hymn much prized, and often sung by the persecuted Christians when scattered by the storm, or fleeing from their foes, or hiding in secret places far off from the friends and the homes they loved. It is now in the Malagasy hymn-book, and from the sacred associations which cluster around it, it will long retain its power over the hearts of Christians in that land. The following is a translation.

"Loud to the Lord your voices raise,
Extol His name, exalt His praise;
Publish the wonders of His hand
O'er all the earth, in every land.

Tell of the pity of the Lord,
Of grace and mercy:—preach the Word;
For wonderful to us appears
That love for us He ever bears.

Though guilty, we're with pardon crown'd;
Condemn'd and lost, we now are found;
Though dead, new life to us is given,
And everlasting life in heaven.

> Oh! God, our God, to Thee we cry,
> Jesus, the Saviour, be Thou nigh;
> Oh! sacred Spirit, hear our prayer,
> And save the afflicted from despair.
>
> Scarce can we find a place for rest,
> Save dens and caves, with hunger press'd;
> Yet thy compassion is our bliss,
> Pilgrims amidst a wilderness."

The day of the martyrdom of these true-hearted sufferers was a peculiarly sorrowful one to the solitary Missionary then at Antananarivo, and to their Christian survivors. Throughout the morning, his heart sunk as the heavy booming of the cannon fell upon his ear, and as he watched the lines of soldiers marching towards the dreaded Ambohipotsy. At noon, officers commissioned by the Queen made the public announcement that nine praying people had been condemned, and would die that day; but it was not until nearly four o'clock that they were led forth from prison. They were then stripped of their clothes, and each of them was slung up to a pole by their hands and feet, which were tightly tied together. In this most painful position, they were borne upon the shoulders of four men to the place of execution. Calm and strong, they endured the torture without murmuring, and when the fatal spot was reached, they showed that death had no terrors for them. Like Rasalama and Rafaralahy, they were sentenced to be speared, and the appointed signal for the execution was the firing of a cannon. All were now awaiting the fatal moment. The match was applied, but the cannon burst, and the gunner was much injured, an accident which the people deemed a bad omen. But the Queen's command admitted of no delay, and as the echoes of the bursting gun were dying away amongst the distant hills, these nine faithful witnessess for Christ were rising to join the noble army of the martyrs, and to take their places in that world where " they hear not the voice of the oppressor." As in the Queen's estimation, Paul and another, whose name is not given, had been more than ordinarily guilty, their heads were cut off and fixed upon poles.

There were still very many, not less than two hundred, "destitute, afflicted, tormented," who "wandered in deserts and in mountains, and in dens and caves of the earth," and whose condition called forth the strong sympathy and solicitude of many British Christians. Intensely anxious for the escape of their persecuted brethren, the Directors of the London Missionary Society instructed their devoted Missionary, Mr. Johns, who continued at the Mauritius principally with this object in view, to spare neither labour nor expense for its attainment. And in that admirable man they possessed an agent in whose judgment, energy, and self-denial they could fully confide. But although he and other friends of the oppressed employed every effort they could devise, the coast was now so closely watched and guarded by the Queen's emissaries, that escape for a single Christian seemed all but hopeless. This was rendered the more distressing from the circumstance that their sufferings and dangers were continually increasing. Many of the Christians had been hunted by the Queen's officers with the instinct and ferocity of bloodhounds, until they had been driven into wild and almost inaccessible heights of the mountains, where there was little shelter and less food. Two of these wanderers risked their lives in visiting a Christian friend at Tamatave, in the hope that some method might be devised for the rescue of their brethren. But with heavy hearts they were compelled to carry back the sad tidings that little or nothing could be done. Wonderful, indeed, was the power of principle, and the energy of Divine grace, which, in circumstances so appalling, made these Christians strong to suffer, and enabled them in the endurance of trial and in the face of death, to "quit themselves like men."

While the two hundred scattered over the country were fleeing from their persecutors, many Christians still remained in and around the capital: but most of these were either prisoners or slaves. The year after Mr. Johns' visit, some of them thus wrote to a friend at Tamatave:—

"Our salutations to you, say the little flock in Madagascar. Through the blessing of God on us, we are yet alive, and do not forget you and all our friends. This is what we have to say to you, beloved Father! The affliction which has occurred to us, and of which you have heard, greatly increases. Executions, ordeals, and miseries increase throughout the country. * * The wretchedness of the people is unutterable. * * Do rescue us, beloved Father! if possible. If God be not our defence, we are dead men. We are as a city set on a hill, that cannot be hid.

"Our Government service continues to be very severe.

When the children of Israel served under Pharaoh, perhaps they obtained some little respite, at any rate, by night; but *ours* is incessant labour! We must work both night and day."

In another letter to the same friend, they say:—"You exhort us to take courage, and not to be cast down. We accept your exhortation, and we all take confidence, and rejoice. And you further ask us if there is any thing we want, adding that we should write and tell you. Now, there is one point on which we are much afflicted—our want of Bibles. We can conceal them, though there are many enemies. Those we have are quite worn out.

"And with regard to the means of our support, it may be said we have, and have not. All our property was taken from us. However, this is the word of the Lord— 'Consider the ravens; they sow not, they reap not, yet God feedeth them.' And just so, dear friend, the Lord has pity on us."

During the next year (1842), the cruelty of the Queen and the constancy of the Christians continued. Five more were at this time added to the honoured roll of Madagascar martyrs. Two of these were on their way back from a place whither they had gone to seek not merely a refuge for themselves and their brethren, but a sphere for evangelistic labour. They belonged to Vonizongo. Their names were Ratsitahina and Rabearahaba. Like many who had suffered before them, they were put to the torture, to extort from their lips the names of their brethren, but the attempt was in vain; all they would acknowledge was that they had themselves prayed, and had followed the practices of the praying people. Just before they suffered, a messenger from their Christian friends found his way to them, to whom they whispered—'Let them not fear that we shall disclose their names. We shall do them no harm; but say farewell! If we do not meet again here on earth, we shall meet in the future life." They were executed in the market-place of Vonizonga, and their heads were stuck upon poles, to warn others not to follow their example.

In a very affecting letter, written about this time, one of the Christians says—"Our trials are greater than ever, and the number of the persecuted is increasing daily. The officers of the Queen are searching for them everywhere, to put them to death. We do not know what to do, as the road in all directions is almost impassable, and our hiding-places are nearly all known to our enemies."

"The present trials of the Christians," writes another, " are very heavy to *flesh and blood*, but they are even light to be borne by the mind and soul that lean upon the Lord. * * I told you, in a former letter, that the Queen ordered the tangena to be given to me, but, by the blessing of God, I got over it. Join me, O my beloved friend! in praising the Lord, who hath blessed and preserved me alive. Five of our friends are hiding themselves with me, and I shall take particular care of them; but others go from place to place to seek for something to support nature."

In October of this year, three more laid down their lives rather than deny the Saviour. Some unknown person had affixed a paper to a wall in Antananarivo, with something written upon it which displeased the Queen. The writer was commanded to give himself up in four days. But as no one obeyed the royal mandate, Raharo, who had been one of the twelve principal teachers in the reign of Radama, was, with other Christians, apprehended upon suspicion. They were forced to drink the tangena, which proved fatal to Raharo. But as another Christian, called Ratsimilay, was detected in an attempt to save his friend from the effects of the poison-cup, he was condemned to die; whilst a third, Imamonjy, was sentenced with him to be cut into small pieces, and then burnt.

Thus far we have sketched the history of eight years of the persecution in Madagascar. Within this short period, hundreds of Christians had been condemned to chains or slavery, while others were hiding in the forests and the mountains, and at least seventeen had suffered death. And for what had they endured such things? For their religion. This was their only crime—their enemies themselves being judges. Had they denied the faith, their property, liberty, and lives would have been safe. A word would have sufficed for this purpose. But no! They took joyfully the spoiling of their goods; they cheerfully endured bonds and imprisonment, and counted not even their lives dear unto themselves, so that they might win Christ, and be found in Him. Such noble virtue, under almost any circumstances, would constrain the thoughtful observer to exclaim—"This is the finger of God!" But this acknowledgment will be made with double emphasis when we consider the history of these heroic sufferers. Had they been nurtured amidst Christian associations, and enjoyed superior advantages of mental and spiritual training, the manifestation of piety like theirs—in circumstances the most trying, and in forms such as have invested with the brightest lustre the most honoured names recorded in the martyrology of the Church—would have constrained us to "glorify God in them." But that such nobleness of character, such triumphs of principle, such superiority to every sordid and selfish motive, such faith in God and fidelity to conscience, such unyielding constancy and unfaltering fearlessness should have been matured and developed in those who from their early days had been surrounded by the dark and debasing influences of paganism, is a phenomenon to baffle philosophers and moralists, and one which admits of none but a Christian solution.

And if any thing more were necessary to prove that God was certainly with them, we might find it in the remarkable fact that, even now, when in the view of sense there was so much to deter others from treading the same path of sorrow and danger, these sufferers could announce that, "the number of learners is greatly increasing," and that several of the people had lately joined them.

Although the Queen's command, enforced by fearful threats, that all books should be delivered up, had been urgent, many of the Christians both in the capital and in the country had disobeyed it, and had hid—often buried— their Bibles in the earth. But the copies thus preserved were few, and many of them had been so diligently read by their possessors, or so often lent to less fortunate friends, that they were almost worn out. What, therefore, they desired above every earthly good, was a supply of this sacred treasure. "Exceedingly afflicted are we," they write, "on account of the fewness of the Bibles here with us, and we exceedingly desire to have more. We are thirsting for them, for the Bible is our companion and friend to instruct, and search in thoroughly, when in secrecy and silence, and to comfort us in our grief and tribulation. Send us *many*, for even then they will not be enough, and let them be small in print, so as to be easily hidden." In the same letter they add—"As to the condition of the country, it is still dark, and there is still persecution by the Queen. Nevertheless, the people are going forward. Blessed be God! who thus prospers them." They further state, that every Saturday the men travel a long distance to some secluded hill or valley, "so as to get beyond the reach of the people, that none may see us, and that we may spend the Sabbath together in worshipping God. But the women are not strong enough to walk so far; and this," add the writers of the letter, "makes us feel very much on account of the sorrow of those who cannot go."

Thus the Christians of Madagascar, though "faint," were "yet pursuing" the pathway of faith and holiness. But still they were often "cast down," and discouraged, and needed the prayer, "Wilt thou not revive us again?" This was especially the case with those in the capital. From the year 1840, that dreadful time when so many had perished, they had been so closely watched that it became increasingly difficult to escape discovery. Since that day, five weary years had rolled along, and still no change had come. God was indeed with them, and His Word was their light in this great darkness. But they were prone to cry, "Why standest thou afar off, O God! Why hidest thou thyself in time of trouble?" And they needed the exhortation, "Consider Him, who endured such contradiction of sinners against Himself, lest ye be weary and faint in your minds."

During the year 1843 the persecuted Christians lost one of their truest and most unwearied friends in Mr. Johns, who fell a sacrifice to fever on the island of Nosibe, whilst endeavouring to find a way of escape for them, and a temporary refuge from the storm. This loss was severely felt by the Directors, who had so long and so justly confided in the zeal, vigilance, and discretion of their invaluable Missionary. But this was only another of the events by which God designed to make His strength perfect and more manifest than ever in the apparent weakness and helplessness of his afflicted people.

A great revival was now at hand. Suddenly, a bright light broke through the black thunder-cloud which had so long hung over the faithful sufferers. At that time there was a youth residing at the capital, named Rainaka. He had become a Christian, and subsequently to the commencement of the persecution, a preacher of the Gospel; and very bold and very earnest he was in the service of the Saviour. Regardless of royal decrees and legal penalties, he laboured with heart and soul to draw others to the Cross. Encouraged by his bright and bold example, three times a week the Christians assembled in a large house for worship. It was a daring venture, but God honoured it. Many strangers were drawn to listen to the young apostle, and not a few of them believed the Gospel. Thus, in a short time about a hundred were added to the proscribed Christians. But this was not all. Amongst these new adherents, there was one of the very last men in Madagascar whom they expected to find there. This was Rakoto-radama (which means *son* of Radama), the Queen's only child, then about seventeen years of age.

In what way the preaching of the zealous Rainaka influenced the young Prince, we do not know; but the good fruits in his character and conduct soon showed themselves, and have continued to this day. Henceforward he was to prove their firm friend and powerful protector. Five months after he had joined the Christians, twenty-one of them were seized by the Queen's order; and as she was much incensed at their boldness and augmented numbers, there is every reason to believe that she had resolved to destroy them all. But now, for the first time, Rakoto placed himself between his heathen mother and his Christian brethren. He went to her and begged for their lives. As she loved her son, his earnest entreaties somewhat softened her hard heart, and saved the accused from death. Nine, however, were compelled to drink the tangena, one of whom died, and the rest were sold as slaves, or kept in chains. But happily, at length by the exertions of the

Prince, they all regained their liberty, though not until those who were imprisoned had been made the instruments of the conversion of their gaolers. How greatly the Christians were encouraged by these wonderful proofs of God's presence and favour, will appear from a letter written by some of them in February 1846, to the Missionaries at Mauritius.

"We went up to Antananarivo, and there met (in a religious assembly) with the Queen's son, and the persecuted Christians, nothing disheartened by the temptations of Satan, though they may suffer in bonds: and those Christians who are not persecuted, we found increasing exceedingly; yea, becoming indeed many. And Rakoto, the Queen's son, makes very great progress in the love of the Lord, by God's blessing, and is able to assemble some Christians with himself every night to thank and praise God. Oh! blessed be God, who has caused His mercy to descend upon Rakoto and all the people!"

From the time when first convinced that the Scriptures were of God, the Prince has continued the fast friend of the Christians, and how valuable that friendship has proved during the dark and stormy years that followed, we shall see. He was cautious, indeed, but he practised no concealment even from his mother. She and others knew perfectly what he was and what he did. He could not indeed openly defy the law, but, wrote the Christians, "He comes regularly with us in the woods on Sundays to pray and sing, and read the Bible; and he often takes some of us home with him to explain to him the Word of Truth, and he keeps his mother from doing us any harm." But just then he was accomplishing even more than this. The printing-press had been long stopped, and was now out of repair. But the Prince employed men to put it again into working order, that it might print the Bible and religious books. This was a very bold proceeding upon his part, and strikingly shows how firm and fearless he was, even though so young. By the great favour of God, the good promise then given has since been, and is now, largely fulfilled.

The agency through which the Prince was first brought into association with the Christians, and then drawn to their secret meetings, appears to have been that of a Christian young man, whose uncle frequented the palace on business, where he was occasionally admitted with him. Influenced, as all the Christians obviously were, by a fervent desire to diffuse the Gospel, this young man contrived to bring the subject under the notice of Rakoto. Thus the interest in Christianity, which, happily for his country, has suffered no decline, was originally awakened in the Prince's mind. Subsequently, the same young disciple drew him to the assemblies of the Christians, where, as already stated, he heard the word of life from the fervid lips of Rainaka.

"From this time," writes one of them, "he was very diligent in conversing with us on the subject of Christianity; and at length he invited some of us into his house in the palace-yard to converse with him in secret, and we were thus frequently invited to his house to converse with him."

It may be well supposed that such a change in Rakoto filled the enemies of Christianity with burning anger, and that many would have rejoiced in his destruction. Amongst those who felt thus was Rainiharo, the chief minister of the Queen. Long had he been the unrelenting foe of the Christians, and well knowing how much they were now protected and encouraged by the Prince, he thirsted for the young man's life, and only waited for a favourable moment to assail it. So one day when alone with the Queen, having, as he imagined, a suitable opportunity for gratifying his wicked desire, he said to her, "Your son, Madam, is a Christian; he prays with the Christians, and encourages them in this new doctrine. We are lost if your Majesty does not stop the Prince in this strange way." "But," replied the Queen, "he is my son, my only, my beloved son! Let him do what he pleases; if he wishes to become a Christian, let him: he is my beloved son!" Thus, happily, the love of the mother proved stronger than the hatred of the persecutor.

But natural affection existed even in Rainiharo himself. This appeared soon afterwards. He had a favourite nephew who had become a Christian, and had attended the secret meetings of the proscribed and hated sect. Without the slightest suspicion of the truth, on one occasion Rainiharo sent this nephew as a spy to one of their well-known resorts, with a strict injunction to record the names of all who were there. To this the nephew made no objection, but instantly hastened to the place where prayer was wont to be made, told the brethren why he had come and who had sent him, and then asked them to separate, lest they should be seen by their foes. On his return home, Rainiharo inquired for the list. "There is none," replied the youth. "Young man!" he sternly exclaimed, "you have disobeyed my orders. Why have you done this? Your head must fall, for you show that you also are a Christian." With simplicity and godly sincerity the nephew said, "Yes, my uncle, I *am* a Christian; and, if you please, you may put me to death, for I pray." The persecutor was confounded at the answer. For a moment he was silent, and gazed with wonder at the youth, who, firm and calm, stood prepared to meet the consequences of his bold confession; but the only reply Rainiharo could make was, "Oh no; you shall not die."

But the son of the sovereign, and the nephew of her chief councillor, were not the only persons of high rank who at that period avowed their attachment to the new religion. Rakoto had a cousin named Ramonja. He was a son of the Queen's sister, and a great favourite of the Queen herself; and it is not improbable that her attachment to him arose, in part at least, from the devotion with which he supported the superstitious customs of the country, and the bitter hostility which, in common with his aunt, he cherished against the Christians; for at this time he was one of their most determined persecutors.

But as there was a close intimacy between him and the

Prince, it was not long ere their conversation turned upon the subject so interesting to both of them, though in so different a way. The result was, that through the efforts of Rakoto, his cousin abandoned the idols and embraced the Gospel, and from that time became the friend and protector of the Christians, and one of the most devout and consistent of their number.

But these conversions were not the only circumstances which at this time cheered the hearts of the Christians. At no previous period had the desire to learn to read been more manifest. But as the teachers subjected themselves to heavy pains and penalties, they very prudently refused to instruct any but those whose character and conduct warranted the belief that they were influenced by love to the Word of God. Yet, notwithstanding this restriction, they tell us that not less than a hundred and fifty of their number were engaged in this work, each of whom was constantly surrounded by pupils, to the number of from six to upwards of twenty.

But there were, at the same time, more decisive proofs of the Divine favour even than this. Early in the year 1847, one of the Christians thus describes their spiritual condition. "How wonderful is the power of God as we see it now in the spirit of anxious inquiry produced in the minds of the people! They come to seek the Lord in the prison with the prisoners, in the hiding-places of the persecuted, in the mountains and in the dingles. Whenever and wherever they can meet with any calling upon the name of the Lord, thither they resort. Sweet are the cords of imprisonment to the prisoners—they are not ashamed of them any longer."

Another writer relates an incident which was not without its influence upon many of the weak and wavering. A heathen man, hoping to bring back the Prince to heathenism, went to him with the grave assurance that if an attempt were made to set fire to the house of the idol Ramahavaly it could not be burned. The Prince resolved that the experiment should be tried, and ordered the keeper of the idol to make the attempt. As, however, he had no wish to be the incendiary, and merely threw a piece of lighted cow-dung upon the roof, which immediately rolled off, the attempt failed. But two Christians forthwith offered themselves for the service, and the work was soon done, the Prince all the while watching the blazing temple from the balcony of his house, and expressing his delight at its destruction.

But while these special indications of the Divine favour sustained the hearts of the Christians at this period, the spirit evinced by their suffering brethren appeared to have communicated itself to them, and to have exerted a powerful influence for good. This will appear from their own communication:—

"Tell all the Churches in your country that we are famishing and hungering for the bread of life. Contrive deep schemes to send us Bibles, for we are as a hundred to one plate at this time, because the books that were formerly received from you have all been burnt.

" The following is our present state :—On the 15th day

of the first month, persecution broke out, and twenty-one were caught: the tangena ordeal was given to nine—eight lived and one died; five were condemned to pay half the value of their persons; five were imprisoned; and two concealed themselves; but these two have made their appearance again, though their judgment has not yet been passed. But the persecution has not prevented the spreading of God's Word, but rather has caused it to spread much more—nay, far and wide. The bonds of the prisoners, the preservation of those tried by the tangena ordeal, the hiding-places of the concealed, and the blood of the martyrs, have facilitated the growth of God's Word in the hearts of men. The hidings of those who conceal themselves bespeak God's power, for they abide under the shadow of the Almighty, not discovered by their enemies, while quite close to them. Why? Because the Lord hides them under the shadow of His wings. When any are condemned to be sold as slaves, none will buy them, because the Lord has softened their hearts; and when any of those that conceal themselves make their appearance, none has strength to accuse and imprison them, for the Lord restraineth the wrath of man.

"The five persons that were in chains remain each in his own house, a watch being set over them; but even those set to guard them do not always remain with them, and the Lord has taken away their chains. Preaching the Word, and mending the Bibles and the small tracts, is the only work they do. A great many people go to talk and converse with them, and even the gaolers who watch them have become Christians. This great power fills the mind of the people with astonishment, and their hearts tell them that there is a God. This is the great power which our eyes are witnessing at present. Therefore, continue in earnest prayers for us and for yourselves.

"Blessed be God, who hath not abandoned us to eternal perdition, but hath sent His beloved Son to redeem us from the bondage of Satan! Yes, the blood of Jesus redeems us, saves us, purifies us, and cleanses us great sinners from all sin. By a great and strong voice has Christ called us, and we have returned to Him. All the brethren and sisters in the faith wish to hear from you, and to have a letter from you as soon as possible.

"One of our beloved brothers in the faith was lately taken ill—his disease became very violent, and the doctor gave him medicines. How wonderfully hath God shown His power in the sickness and recovery of this brother! The God of Heaven collected the brethren and sisters in Christ to come and see him, and nurse him in his sickness. He did not cease to speak of the goodness of the Lord, while every one wondered that he could speak at all, owing to the violence of his disease: when the Christians would come to see him he seemed as happy as if he had no disease upon him. The love of the Christians was kindled into a flame by hearing him talking as freely as if he were in a country where there is no hindrance to the truth. The believers seeing this, rejoiced and praised God for what He had done *to* him and *for* him. We had no hopes of his recovery, but, blessed be God, he is restored to us. All were amazed, and exclaimed, 'God alone maketh alive.' This sickness caused many to come forward and inquire the way to eternal life. Our sick brother is now restored to health and strength. May you live and be happy! may you be greatly blessed of God!"

From other letters written from the years 1845 to 1847, but their precise dates are unknown, the following passages are extracted, as exhibiting the inward power and life, as well as the outward circumstances, of the Christians at this period:—

"With regard to our condition here, we are well; but two sisters the 'Lord has taken away,' and another, the wife of one of us. So far as we can judge respecting their removal, it is happy; for we indulge the hope that God has received them through the salvation which is in Christ: 'Blessed are the dead who die in the Lord;' and wonderful indeed is the blessing of God; for He has truly answered our prayer and your cries; so that, as to ourselves, not any of us have been apprehended by the persecution.

"The number of the learners is very greatly increasing; and those who were reduced to slavery, 'never to be redeemed,' have been permitted to be redeemed. Yes; wonderful and astonishing altogether is the power of God, for He rescues His people from the hands of the wicked. He redeemed Israel from slavery, and He plucks them from the hand of the devil, that they may become the people of God. Read Acts v. 39.

"Be, therefore, strong in prayer for us, O friends! Tell

all your companions, as widely as you can, that 'what is not possible with men is possible with God,' and 'none can hinder what He does.' Do not be unmindful of the children that God has given to be nursed and trained by you, for God will not be unmindful of you; and He will do still more abundantly! Therefore, be earnest in prayer, O beloved! for prayer is power, and strength, and life; for God hears your supplications there, and sends his answers to us. We earnestly desire to have some spelling-books and reading-lessons. * * * *

"And now, in conclusion, O beloved! when we examine the Word of God from the beginning to the end, and the passages which are suitable to us in the Word, it gives us hope and confidence indeed. We see that God is powerful; that no one can pluck out of His hands, nor hinder that which He is doing. Read, if you please, Daniel iii. 27, 28; iv. 34, 35; vi. 20, 28. Earnestly, therefore, plead on our account and your own; for, if God be with us, who can be against us? (Romans viii. 31—39.)

"To beloved friends, kindest salutations from all your companions. This is what we have to tell you.

"And we desire also books of instruction—hymns, spelling books, catechisms, and John Bunyan; and if there are any tracts, such as are suitable for us, they can be divided among us; and so also of anything that is new, so that we may see it; as Jesus said to Peter, 'Feed my sheep.'

"And as to the condition of our country, it is still dark, and there is still persecution by the Sovereign. Nevertheless, the people are going forward. Blessed be God!

who thus prospers them. And with regard to ourselves, on the Sabbath-day we always go to some hill or valley, far away from the multitude. However, though our sorrow be thus great, still we do not faint, but continue to ask of God that He may help us not to become faint amidst affliction, for Jesus says, Matt. x. 38—'Whosoever will not take up his cross and follow me, is not worthy of me;' and He also says, John xvii. 33—'These things have I spoken unto you that ye may have life in me. In the world ye shall have tribulation; but be of good cheer, I have overcome the world.'

"All our friends who were reduced to slavery have been redeemed. Blessed be God! He is the Ruler of the world, and He has given the disposition to let the captives go free. We are going on safely, for God has hidden us beneath the shadow of His wings, so that we have not been observed by the people. And yet many do see us, and they know, and hear about us, but they do not now come forward to impeach us, saying, 'These pray,' for even the people around us have become compassionate towards us. And we all send our salutations to all friends."

Thus, by various indications of His presence and grace, God was not only sustaining and reviving the hearts of His servants, but preparing them for trial more terrible than any which they had hitherto endured—the great persecution of 1849. And amongst the exciting causes to which that persecution must be traced, are those which had brought the greatest gladness to their hearts—the manifest and marvellous proofs of progress and prosperity. These, so cheering to themselves, were hateful to their foes. The increasing numbers and boldness of the Christians; the openness with which they assembled, and read and prayed in defiance of law; and still more the fact that her son, her nephew, and others of high rank had embraced their opinions, attended their meetings, and aided their escape from punishment, filled the Queen and her abettors with rage almost amounting to madness. It is at this period that Rambosalama, the brother of Ramonja, first comes prominently into view. Adopted by the Queen as her successor to the throne prior to the birth of her son, this young man had always regarded Rakoto as his enemy and supplanter. He had long been opposed to the new religion; but the Prince's adhesion to it increased his hostility, and made him, there is reason to believe, a chief instigator of the persecution of 1849, as well as an active agent in the discovery and impeachment of Christians. He sent spies in all directions, and employed other means which proved but too effectual in bringing suffering upon the objects of his aversion.

The earliest indication of the coming tempest appeared on the 19th of February, 1849, in an order from the Queen to destroy two houses which had been used for Christian worship. Prince Ramonja interposed a claim upon one of them, but it was disregarded, and the buildings were razed to the ground. During the next two days, nine Christians were consigned to prison. One of these had been an officer of the army, and after the loss of his sight, had become a preacher of the Gospel. Fearless and faithful, this good man and two of his companions embraced the opportunity of urging the truth of God upon the attention and conscience of the high officers who visited them in prison, and others to whom they had access.

In the course of the following week, the people were twice called together to a kabary; and when they were assembled, an officer thus addressed them: "'I ask you,' saith the Queen 'what is the reason you will not forsake the very root of this new religion and mode of worship? For I have deprived officers of their honour, put some to death, reduced others to unredeemable slavery, and you still persevere in practising this new religion. What is the reason why you will not renounce it and deliver up the books by which you have done this?'" Bold must they have been who could answer these words of the Queen. But such there were amongst the Christians, two of whom thus replied in the name of their companions: "We are restrained by reverence for God and His law!" It was a noble reply, and was influenced by the same spirit which constrained the apostolic appeal, "whether it be right in the sight of God to hearken unto you more than unto God, judge ye."

But all the recorded confessions made by the Christians at this time breathe the same spirit. "When," said one, "the Queen inquires why we have not abandoned this worship, we reply that there is a law in this worship, which makes us afraid of God if we steal, or if we commit murder, or if we deceive our fellows, or if we do any evil. *There-fore we have not forsaken it.*" "We make supplication," said another, "to God for the Queen, for her subjects, for our wives and children, and for all the good we need, and as we can do this, we have not forsaken the religion."

Nine Christians who had refused to take the prescribed oath were wrapped in mats and loaded with chains; to this number an officer of the army and a soldier were added shortly afterwards. On being again urged to submit to the Queen, they unitedly refused, and added, "It is God that we worship, for He, and He only, can do all things for us, and we will pray to none but Him."

Immediately after this, five others were accused, two of them attendants upon Prince Ramonja. One of these attendants, named Ramany, stood up before the multitude, and, in reply to the Queen's demand that he would renounce the Gospel and take the idolatrous oaths which she had prescribed, said, with a courage and calmness like that of the martyr Stephen, "I believe in God, for He alone can do all things for me; but as for swearing by the Queen, or by one's mother or sister, or father or brother, a lie is a lie still, whether you swear to it or not. I believe in God, and put my trust in Jesus Christ, the Saviour and Redeemer of all that believe in Him." He and his companions were then loaded with chains, and cast into prison.

The following account of the examination of some of these witnesses for Christ was given to Mr. Ellis.

"Do you pray to the sun, or the moon, or the earth?" asked the officer.

"I do not pray to these," was the answer, "for the hand of God made them."

Officer. "Do you pray to the twelve sacred mountains?"

Christian. "I do not pray to them, for they are mountains."

O. "Do you pray to the idols that render sacred the Kings?"

C. "I do not pray to them, for the hand of man made them."

O. "Do you pray to the ancestors of the sovereigns?"

C. "Kings and rulers are given by God, that we should serve and obey them, and render them homage. Nevertheless, they are only men like ourselves. When we pray, we pray to God alone."

O. "You make distinct, and observe the Sabbath day?"

C. "That is the day of the great God; for in six days the Lord made all His works. But God rested on the seventh, and He caused it to be holy; and I rest, to keep sacred that day."

There are some things in these confessions which deserve special notice. Had there been at that most exciting time, and amongst a people so recently brought out of darkness so dense into light so marvellous, left as they now were without the counsels and aid of the men from whom they had received the Gospel, some indications of ill-regulated zeal, an undue desire for a martyr's crown, or a low estimate of life and of death, we might not have been surprised. But never have sufferers evinced less of irrational enthusiasm. Theirs was "a loving sacrifice,"—"a reasonable service."

While using every justifiable precaution to evade the threatened penalties, they resorted to no unworthy arts of concealment or compromise. And in all their answers to the royal requirements, we clearly discover that the will of Christ was their only law. Each could truly say, " But so did not I because of the fear of God." Hence the simplicity and strength with which they assigned the reasons of their refusal. Nor should those reasons themselves be unnoticed. Independently of other sources of information, their accusers make it evident that the only crime ever alleged against them was their Christianity. Their worst foes could " find no occasion against them except concerning the law of their God." Upon this point the testimony is the most explicit. In all the Queen's edicts their evil practices are minutely described. The following is a specimen of many similar documents, and contains the worst that could be said of these Christian confessors.

" These are the things which shall not be done, saith the Queen. The saying to others, Believe and obey the Gospel; the practice of baptism; the keeping of the Sabbath as a day of rest; the refusing to swear by one's father, or mother, or sister, or brother; and the refusing to be sworn, with a stubbornness like that of bullocks, or stones, or wood; and refusing to fight and quarrel, the taking of a little bread and the juice of the grape, and asking a blessing to rest on the crown of your heads; and kneeling down upon the ground and praying, and rising from prayer with drops of water falling from your noses, and with tears rolling down from your eyes."

When we consider, in the light thus thrown upon it, the character of these Christians, we can understand why it was when bonds, imprisonment, tortures and death awaited them, that they denied nothing, concealed nothing, and feared nothing. Nor is it wonderful that others who saw their boldness "took knowledge of them that they had been with Jesus." The husband of one, a pious woman who was bound at this time, was so impressed with what he heard, that he came up to the prisoners and said—" Be not afraid, for it is well if for that you die." Upon this, he too was apprehended, and having confessed his faith in Christ, was bound, and led away with the others.

Nineteen Christians now lay under sentence of death, and their brethren knew that their execution was fixed for the morrow. What could they do for them? Let us observe their proceedings.

The midnight hour has closed a day of terror, and yet of triumph to the Christians—one of the darkest, but one of the brightest in the history of Madagascar. Though the city is still, here and there individuals and groups might have been seen quietly leaving their dwellings and stealing noiselessly along the streets. Whither are they going? The word has passed from lip to lip that they are to meet to pray for their suffering brethren. "And at one at night," writes one of those who were present, and who took part in the service, "we met together, and prayed." What meaning is there in these simple words, and what power was there in the exercise they describe! Had we listened, as these devout men, with strong cryings and tears, sought aid for their beloved brethren from Him who was able to succour and to save, how assured should we have felt that in answer to such supplications the Divine arm would be stretched out on their behalf!

For evidence that thus it was, we have only to visit other spots, and gaze upon other scenes which have made that day memorable in Madagascar history, and which will cause it to be had in everlasting remembrance. The voice of prayer as it rose from the assembled believers had scarcely died away, and the light of morning had not yet appeared, when the city was all astir. Swiftly and widely had the intelligence spread on the previous evening that the decree of the Queen had gone forth, and that on the following day nineteen Christians would suffer; and great was the multitude which now hastened to the spots where these noble martyrs would demonstrate the sincerity of their faith in Jesus, and the strength of their love to His cause, by following Him in the same path of suffering which He trod, and laying down their lives for His sake.

There were two spots to be rendered almost sacred by the sufferings and the spirit of those who were there cruelly sacrificed upon that day. One is called ARAPIMARINANA. The meaning of the name is, "the place of hurling down." It is in the midst of the city, and the place of execution is a precipice of granite 150 feet high, over which condemned persons were flung. Hither, on this dreadful morning, flowed the stream of people: some prompted by the desire of excitement, others by their hatred to the Christians, but many, no doubt, by deep sympathy; and here, crowding the dreadful spot almost to the edge of the giddy precipice, stood the gathered throng. But let us turn from them to the prison. Meek, like their Divine Master, though seized with rude violence and flung upon the ground, no complaint escapes the sufferers' lips. But far different sounds are heard. As they sit upon the ground, with heart and voice they unite in singing a favourite hymn, which thus begins:

> " When I shall die, and leave my friends,
> When they shall weep for me,
> When departed has my life,
> Then I shall happy be!"

And when that hymn was ended, they began another, the first line of which is—

" When I shall, rejoicing, behold Him in the heavens."

But these sounds of sacred melody were now drowned by the hoarse, harsh voice of the Queen's messenger, who, in the name of Ranavalona, is pronouncing upon each the sentence they were that day to suffer. Four of them were nobles, two of whom were husband and wife. As it was unlawful to shed the blood of persons of their rank, they were to be burned alive, and the remaining fifteen[*] to be thrown from "the place of hurling down." As the officer was leaving the prison, the nobles sent a request to the Queen that they might be strangled before their bodies

---

[*] Mr. Ellis speaks of eighteen, but the compiler has followed the authority of native letters written at the time, from which it appears that fourteen suffered, and that one, a young female, was saved.

were burned; but even such mercy was denied. The fifteen, wrapped in mats, and with mats thrust into their mouths to prevent their speaking to each other, or to the people, were then hung by their hands and feet to poles, and carried to the place of execution. But the attempt wholly to stop their mouths failed, for they prayed and addressed the crowd as they were borne along. "And some," we are told, "who beheld them, said that their faces were like the faces of angels."

Thus they reached ARAPIMARINANA. A rope was then firmly tied round the body of each, and one by one, fourteen of them were lowered a little way over the precipice. While in this position, and when it was hoped by their persecutors that their courage would fail, the executioner, holding a knife in his hand, stood waiting for the command of the officer to cut the rope. Then for the last time the question was addressed to them, "Will you cease to pray?" But the only answer returned was an emphatic "No." Upon this the signal was given, the rope was cut, and in another moment the mangled and bleeding body lay upon the rocks below. One of those brave sufferers for Christ, whose name was Ramonambonina, as he was led to the edge of the precipice, begged his executioners to give him a short time to pray, "for on that account," he said, "I am to be killed." His request being granted, he kneeled down and prayed aloud very earnestly; and having risen from his knees he addressed the people with such powerful and subduing eloquence that all were amazed and many struck with awe. Then turning to his executioners, he said, "My *body* you will cast down this precipice; but my *soul* you cannot, as it will go up to heaven to God. Therefore it is gratifying to me to die in the service of my Maker."

What the people thought and said as they left that spot and returned to their homes we are not told, but who can doubt that from that hour the truth of the religion of Jesus was more clearly seen, and its power more deeply felt by some than it had been before.

Mr. Ellis and the Bishop of Mauritius visited this spot, and the latter thus refers to it:—

"It was a very harrowing spectacle to witness the actual rock from which our brethren and sisters have been thrown with so much cruelty to meet so fearful a death; but the evidence was clear that they died with unfailing faith and triumphant hope. The brother of one of the sufferers was with us—a manly and devoted Christian he seemed to be. I saw him every day, I believe, while I was in Antananarivo, and sometimes twice a day and oftener. He brought his children to see me, and from all that I saw of him, I was led to form the highest opinion of his straightforward earnest, Christian character; but, when he afterwards came to the spot to which the bodies had been taken to be burnt, he wept like a child at the recollection of his brother's sufferings. One severe part of the fiery trial through which these Christians passed on to their rest with God, was their being placed where they could see the fall of their brethren, and then being asked whether they would not recant. All such attempts to move them proved ineffectual. They seemed so filled with the love of their Saviour, and with joyful hope of heaven, that they utterly despised all offers of life on such conditions. One very striking instance I heard of from an old officer of the palace, as well as from our companions on that day. A young woman who was very beautiful and accomplished and who was very much liked by the Queen, was placed where she could see her companions fall, and was asked, at the instance of the Queen—who wished to save her, but could not exempt her from the common sentence against the Christians—whether she would not worship the gods, and save her life. She refused, manifesting so much determination to go with her brethren and sisters to heaven, that the officer standing by struck her on the head, and said, 'You are a fool! you are mad!' And they sent to the Queen and told her that she had lost her reason, and should be sent to some place of safe keeping. She was sent away, strongly guarded, into the country, some thirty miles, and afterwards was married to a Christian man, and died only two years ago, leaving two or three children behind her."

But there is another place where martyrs of Jesus are to suffer on this fatal day. Its name is FARAVOHITRA, which means "the last village." Let our readers mark it well. The King of Madagascar has given it, and three other spots consecrated by the blood of the martyrs, as the sites of Memorial Churches in memory of the martyrs. And here it is proposed that the Church shall be built by the Young People of Great Britain and Ireland, and that it shall proclaim to the present and to future generations of Madagascar their veneration for those who suffered there.

Faravohitra stands high on the crest of a hill on the northern part of Antananarivo, and what took place there on this memorable day could be seen from a large part of the city. As it was well known that four Christian nobles were to be burned alive, a crowd surrounded the spot, and watched, with varied feelings, the preparations for the horrid execution. The stakes were firmly fixed in the ground, fuel was piled up around them, and the grim executioners stood ready for their dreadful work. Instead, however, of being carried on poles, like their humbler brethren, it would appear that these titled sufferers were allowed to walk to the place of execution. And how great, how triumphant their faith! There was no wavering, no shrinking back from the fiery ordeal. Even the Christian lady, who had peculiar reasons for dreading the flames, was raised above all weakness and fear. And as they went along, they sang together a hymn, which begins with

"When our hearts are troubled,"

and each verse of which ends with

"Then remember us."

They reached the place, calmly gazed upon the preparations for their death, and meekly surrendered themselves to be fastened to the stakes. "At the moment when they were brought to the stakes," writes an eye-witness, "a remarkable phenomenon occurred. A rainbow of an immense size, and forming a triple arch, stretched across the heavens. One end of it appeared to the spectators to rest on the posts to which the martyrs were tied. The rain in the meanwhile fell in torrents; and the multitudes who were present on the occasion were so struck with amazement and terror at the occurrence that many of them took to flight."

The pile was kindled, and then, from amidst the crackling and roaring of the fire, were heard, not the sounds of pain, but the song of praise. That scene, and the hymn which these martyrs sung as they rose in their fiery chariot to heaven, will never be forgotten in Madagascar. But prayer followed praise. "O Lord," they were heard to cry, "receive our spirits; for Thy love to us has caused this to come to us; and lay not this sin to their charge!"

"Thus," writes a witness of that wonderful and memorable scene, "they prayed, as long as they had any life. Then they died; but softly—gently. Indeed, gently was the going forth of their life, and astonished were all the people around, that beheld the burning of them there."

But while this tragic scene is being acted in Faravohitra another is in progress. As the cruel orders of the Queen, in hurling the fourteen martyrs from the precipice of Arapimarinana had been obeyed, we might have supposed that even her malignity would have been fully satisfied. But no! not yet. Hastening to the spot where lie their mangled bodies, in some of which possibly life's expiring flame still trembled, officers seize the ropes which hung around them, and then, followed by the rabble with yells and execrations, they drag them through the streets of the city to the spot where the four nobles had suffered. Feeding the fires afresh which had consumed those honoured servants of Christ, body after body was flung upon the pile, until the horrid work had been consummated.

And now pause and think awhile. Here are Heathenism and Christianity face to face. "Look on this picture and on that!" See human nature without the Gospel: see it with! Contrast the passions of the Queen and her agents —their bitter malice and fiendish ferocity—with the sweet smiles and sacred songs of the burning nobles, and ask, Who? what, has made them to differ? Their own explanation is the only one. It is "by the grace of God." Nothing less is sufficient; nothing more is necessary. Lately, Mr. Ellis surveyed the place where these things were done, and speaking of FARAVOHITRA, he thus writes:—

"When I visited the place in company with the Bishop of Mauritius, we stood and gazed on the prisons in the distance, in which the sufferers had been confined, on the place where their sentences were read over to them, and where as they sat together on the ground, bound with chains, and encircled by soldiers, they sang their hymn of praise to Christ. We passed up the road along which, surrounded by an excited crowd, they raised their voices in prayer that God would remember them. We stood by the side of the spot—the place itself we felt to be holy ground—on which, when fastened to the stake, they sang—

> 'There is a blessed land,
> Making most happy;
> Never (thence) shall rest depart,
> Nor cause of sorrow come.'

"Our companions, most of whom had been spectators on that eventful day, and one the brother of a martyr, pointed out where the soldiers and the heathen stood around and cried, 'Where is Jehovah now? Why does He not come and take you away?' To which, from the midst of the flames, the martyrs answered, 'Jehovah is here; he is taking us to a better place.' Our companions also showed us the part of the road, a little distant, on which the relatives and associates of the Christians stood, waving their last adieus to their rejoicing friends, who smiled, and lifted up as far as they could, their scorched hands or burning fragments of dress, to return the salutation. In perfect accordance with this account is the spirit and feeling manifested by survivors when recounting their sufferings. I have sometimes sat as if enchained to the lips of the venerable widow or sister of a martyr, as she has recounted with simple pathos the suffering she has endured; and have been overcome with wonder and admiration at the marvellous power of 'the love of Christ shed abroad in their hearts by the Holy Ghost given unto them.' The Christians especially rejoice in a proposal to raise, as a perpetual memorial of these events, a church consecrated to the worship of the martyr's God and Saviour."

In another letter, Mr. Ellis adds, "The deep emotion with which the Pastors and others spoke on this topic was most affecting. Some, they said, had lost fathers, others children, some wives, others husbands, or brothers, or sisters, whom they now rejoiced to think of as with the spirits of just men made perfect in heaven, but whom they and their fellow Christians would never forget. If churches, they said, were built upon the spots on which they had suffered and died for the love of Christ, it would not only comfort surviving friends but do much to perpetuate the impressions which their constancy had produced upon the minds of both Christians and heathens."

But while, for a brief space, our earnest thought is naturally fixed upon those who, in this fiery persecution, died for Christ, we must not overlook the far larger number who at the same time were condemned to suffer in the same cause. Thirty-seven preachers, with their wives and families, were consigned to a life of slavery. More than a hundred were flogged with the whip, and sentenced to work in chains during their lives. Some who were made slaves might purchase back their liberty and the liberty of their wives and children, if money enough could be found, but the slavery of others was irredeemable. Many were heavily fined, and those who had been among the great and noble of the land were stripped of their honours and titles, and not only reduced in rank, but forced to the hardest and meanest labour. Altogether, in the early spring of 1849—that fearful year which the Christians truly called the year of "the great persecution"—1903, according to the lowest estimate, but more probably upwards of 2000 were punished, because they had either professed or favoured the religion of Jesus.

Some who had been officers in the army were reduced to the rank of common soldiers, and to enhance their punishment, they were condemned to build a stone house.

This, especially for men altogether unused to such severe manual labour, was a most painful task, as they were compelled, with rude tools, to dig out the blocks of stone from the quarry, to square them, and to carry them to the site of the building. Hard-hearted taskmasters too were placed over them; their clothing was bare, and their food short; but on and on for a whole year they were compelled to toil. And besides this, they were branded with the name, "Tsihiaharana," which means, "That which is not to be imitated," and which was given to them that others who witnessed their sufferings might be deterred from obeying the Gospel. Nor was this all. As soon as they had completed one heavy task, they were called to others equally laborious. Thus, after the house had been built, they were sent into the forest to fell trees, and as there were neither conveyances nor roads, they were compelled to drag them through the jungle, and over hill and dale to a considerable distance. Some were despatched to fight the Sakalaves, and were required to remain in the enemy's country during the wet season, while victims to deadly fever were falling on every hand. One of these Christians thus writes:—"I was condemned to slavery, and valued at thirty dollars. My wife and children were also made slaves. My property was all taken from me. I was aide-de-camp to Rainiharo, and had been promoted to the eighth honour.* . But mine honour was taken from me, and I was made a common soldier, to carry a musket, and perform the exercise of a

---

* About equal to that of a Colonel in the British army.

soldier once every fortnight, until my skin peeled off, like that of a serpent, every time we performed the exercise; for we were not allowed to wear either a hat or a shirt, but only a girdle around our loins. 'Blessed be God who lightens our sorrows.'" 2 Cor. v.

Amongst those who were condemned at this time, was the Prince Ramonja. Though a favourite of his aunt, he was sentenced to pay a heavy fine, and to be stripped of his honours. But he suffered all with Christian meekness. No man was more deservedly beloved and honoured by his brethren than he. His house became their meeting and sometimes their hiding-place, and most cheerfully did he expend his remaining property in providing for those who had been robbed of their all. "He is a wise man," writes one who had experienced his help, "and truly loves Christ. He fights the good fight every day. He preaches constantly to the Queen, though her heart kindles against him whenever he opens his mouth on the subject of Christianity. * * * He is at present called to bear greater affliction, and to carry a heavier cross than any of the Christians; but he considers all this light, and preaches the word boldly, and continually to the Queen and to his relations. He does not mind the rage of his sovereign's heart against him, but we, his companions, are very sorry for what he has been called to endure. His relations often upbraid him for what he suffers. 'He does not follow the religion of his ancestors, but he follows the religion of the ancestors of the white people, and that is the reason of his afflictions.' But the Prince speaks to them, saying, 'I do *not* worship the ancestors of strangers, nor my own ancestors, but God, that made heaven and earth: Him alone do I worship; and Jesus Christ, who died for the sins of men.' They consider him on this account obstinate, but the Queen does not punish him, because he is her sister's beloved son."

If the fear of pain, privation, and death could have shaken the faith and courage of the Madagascar Christians, their numbers and influence would assuredly have been greatly diminished after this terrible trial; but none of these things moved them. They encouraged themselves and each other in the Lord, and were sustained by the conviction that the day of their deliverance would come. Secretly, therefore, and steadily, they travelled on in the path of duty, though it was oftentimes a way of darkness and difficulty. Fearless of consequences, they still assembled for worship. And there were now seven houses in the capital, and others in the country, where, under the shadow of night, they met to consider Him whose love for them was stronger than death, and to speak and hear of that world where "the wicked cease from troubling, and the weary are at rest." In this they were countenanced by the example of the Prince Royal, of Ramonja, and of others high in rank, who were ready to lay their honours and their lives at the Saviour's feet. And after a time some appeared in their solemn assemblies whom they were both surprised and delighted to welcome. These were beloved brethren who had found their way back to the capital, from which they had been banished. Still they were "prisoners of the Lord," and in bonds. Each of them bore the heavy iron fetters that had been from the first rivetted upon their limbs; and a strange spectacle must they have presented to the Christians as they entered their meetings, and very sad the sound of their clanking chains, as they returned the salutations of their brethren, or lifted their fettered hands to God in prayer. But doubtless the courage and constancy they had shown, cheered the hearts and confirmed the faith of many who saw that though "persecuted" they were "not forsaken."

There were others at these private gatherings who had suffered the loss of all things. The imposition of fines had left them penniless. But this only furnished occasion for new manifestations of Christian principle and affection. It might almost be said that, like primitive believers, they had all things common. This, at least, is certain, that the noble man who now reigns, his devout cousin, and others of the more wealthy Christians expended nearly all their property in assisting their destitute brethren.

The chief cause of the unyielding firmness of these Christian confessors was their simple faith in God's Word, their familiar acquaintance with its contents, and the deep love with which they regarded it. Most truly was it their meditation day and night, the man of their counsel, a light to their feet and a lamp to their path, more precious to them than thousands of gold and silver. But that Word was scarce. Many copies of it had been given up, and others had been discovered by the diligent search of the Queen's officers. Only a few had been preserved. These were hidden or buried until they could be safely brought forth for the edification of the brethren, many of whom were destitute of this treasure. But these heard it read, or borrowed it for a season, and in this way they richly stored their memories with its contents. The letters written to the Missionaries after their departure are replete with indications of their extensive and accurate acquaintance with the sacred page, for scarcely a statement or a sentiment occurs which they do not support by Scripture references.

The Directors, and their friends at Mauritius, made repeated and strenuous attempts to satisfy the cravings of the Christians for Bibles, but the obstacles were so formidable that few copies could be added to their scanty stock.

Describing his first visit to Tamatave, Mr. Ellis says that nothing struck him so much as the earnest, repeated, and importunate applications for the Scriptures, and Christian books, which reached him from all quarters. "One finelooking young officer," he writes, in a letter to the Directors, "who had come from a distance, on hearing that we were at Tamatave, almost wept, when, in reply to his earnest request for a book, Mr. Cameron told him that he had not a single copy left."

While Mr. Ellis was at Mauritius, he received a letter from a Christian who had nearly lost his sight, in consequence of having devoted years in copying portions of Scripture for his Christian brethren.

One evening while at Tamatave, two men called at Mr. Ellis's house. On being admitted, they told him that, having heard that he had brought the Bible to their land, they had travelled a long distance in order to get a copy. As they were strangers to him, he thought that possibly they might be spies, and that if he complied with their request, he might be banished from the island. He told them, therefore, that he could not give them what they wanted then, but that they might call upon him again on the following morning. In the meantime, he made inquiries about them from some of the Christians of the place, and learned that they were excellent men, and members of a family that feared the Lord greatly; that they lived at the capital, and having come down about a hundred and fifty miles towards the coast on business, and having there heard that Mr. Ellis was at Tamatave with the Word of God, they resolved to travel more than a hundred miles further, in the hope that they might secure this treasure for themselves. Of course Mr. Ellis was delighted to hear such a report of these worthy men, and was ready, when they came again on the following morning, to give them what they wanted. Before doing this, however, he learned from them that their family was large and scattered, but that all of the members of it were Christians. When asked whether they had the Scriptures, they told Mr. Ellis that they had seen them and heard them, but that all they possessed were " some of the words of David," which, however, did not belong to themselves alone, but to the whole family. He further ascertained that this sacred fragment was sent from one to another, and that each, after keeping it for a time, passed it on, until it had been read by all. Mr. Ellis then inquired whether they had these "words of David" with them. This was a question which they seemed unwilling to answer; but at length they confessed that they had. Mr. Ellis having requested to see the book, they looked at one another, and appeared as if they knew not what to do. At length one of them thrust his hand deep into his bosom, and from beneath the folds of his lamba drew forth a parcel. This he very slowly and carefully opened. One piece of cloth after another having been gently unrolled, at length there appeared a few leaves of the Book of Psalms, which the good man cautiously handed to Mr. Ellis. Though it was evident that the greatest care had been taken of them, their soiled appearance, worn edges, and other marks of frequent use, showed plainly enough how much they had been read. We can only fancy the feelings with which our friend looked upon these few dingy and well-worn leaves, revealing as they did the deep love their possessors felt for God's Word, and the diligence with which they kept and used it. Desiring to possess these precious fragments, Mr. Ellis asked the men whether they had not seen other words of David besides those which they now produced, and also the words of Jesus, and of Paul, of Peter, and of John? Yes, they replied, they had seen them and heard them read, but did not possess them. "Well, then," said Mr. Ellis, holding out the tattered leaves, "if you will give me these few words of David, I will give you *all* his words, and I will give you besides, the words of Jesus, and of John, and of Paul, and of Peter." Upon this he handed to them a copy of the New Testament and the Psalms bound together, and said, "You shall have all these if you will give me this." The men were at first amazed. Then they compared the Psalms they had with those in the book, and having satisfied themselves that all their own words of David were in it, with many more, and that beside these there were other Scriptures which they greatly desired, light beamed in their faces, they took Mr. Ellis at his word, gave him those leaves of the Book of Psalms which had so long yielded them comfort, seized the volume he offered in exchange, bade him farewell, and hastily left the house. In the course of the day he inquired after them, wishing to speak to them again, when the Christians at Tamatave told him that as soon as they left his house, they set out upon their long journey to the capital, doubtless "rejoicing as one that findeth great spoil."

For two or three years after the great persecution, there was a lull in the tempest. But this was not the effect of any change in the Queen's feelings towards her Christian subjects. "Her wrath," writes one of them, in 1852, "continues to rage against us, for there is a law written in a book, stating, 'That no person is allowed to pray and worship according to the religion of the white people. He that does that shall be put to death,' saith the sovereign. 'The worship and religion of my ancestors you must follow and practise for ever and ever, but the worship or religion of any other people shall never be allowed in my country,' saith the Queen. This law is read every fortnight to the soldiers when they are exercised."

But though still "breathing out threatenings and slaughter against the disciples of the Lord," her violence was at this time restrained. This, doubtless, may be ascribed in part to the influence of her son, to the Prince Ramonja, and to other Christian nobles, with whose assistance in the conduct of the Government she could not dispense. But the principal cause was the death of Rainiharo, her chief minister and great favourite. From the commencement of the persecution, this implacable man had been forward to advise, and execute the most severe measures against the hated Christians, and in him the Queen ever found a ready instrument of her will. But the close of his direful career gave the Christians a brief respite from persecution, and awakened a hope that their deliverance drew nigh. What confirmed this hope was the fact that Roharo, Rainiharo's son, who was a friend of the Prince, and now, through Rakoto's influence, commander of the forces, had joined himself to them. Nor was this all. Left without her chief counsellor, and feeling the effects of age and disease, the Queen from this time leaned more than ever upon her son, and, to some extent, shared the Government with him. In 1853, indeed, it was believed that she had resolved to abdicate in his favour; and this was so positively stated that the Directors appealed to their friends for the means of resuming the Mission, and sent Messrs. Ellis and Cameron to Madagascar to employ such measures as might be necessary for this purpose. But these hopes were not realized. Nevertheless, the intelligence obtained by Mr. Ellis, both on this and two subsequent visits, was not only of great value, but such as justified the conclusion that the time to favour Madagascar was at hand.

Mr. Ellis's admirable volume is so well known, that it may suffice to state, that during the month he passed at the capital on his third visit, in 1856, his intercourse with the Christians of all classes, and the information he obtained from them, proved of inestimable value. Referring to them, shortly after his return, Mr. Ellis thus spoke:— "With regard to the Christians, language would fail me to express the grateful joy with which they heard of my arrival, the messages of welcome greeting they sent to me along the road, the manner in which they came out, not one day's, or two days', or three days' journey to meet me on my way, and to ask after the brethren and sisters in England, the progress of the kingdom of Christ in this our native land, and the interest that was felt there in the progress of the Gospel. And when I told them of the untiring affection of British Christians, and their unremitting prayer in their behalf, they wept with joy, and on one occasion they said, 'We cannot make answer—let us kneel down and pray;" and all knelt down together, and one of the native pastors of a native church offered up their thanksgivings to the Most High." "Their numbers," he added, "may be estimated by thousands; and not only are their numbers so great, but their character, their quality, their standard of Christian excellence, would suffer nothing by the most minute and rigid comparison with the purest Churches of our own country."

Still no change had passed over the spirit of the Queen,

and yet there appeared reason to hope that severe measures against the Christians would not be renewed. These calculations, however, proved to be unfounded. Another time of great trouble was at hand, as great as any that had preceded it. The full particulars of this persecution have not as yet been ascertained, but the following brief statement will indicate its origin and its consequences.

For some years there had been a few French residents at Antananarivo, who, by their mechanical knowledge and mercantile transactions, had made themselves useful to the Government. One of these had been settled there for several years. These men, under the pretext of delivering the country from the cruelties and oppression of Ranavalona, determined to dethrone her, and to establish a "French Protectorate"—that false and fraudulent misnomer for French usurpation and Popish intolerance. By their promises and persuasions, they had gained over several men of rank and influence, and had also secreted in one of their own houses a large quantity of arms, armour, and ammunition. Everything having been arranged, the night was fixed upon during which the palace was to be invaded, the Queen seized, and the new Government proclaimed. But Ranavalona was apprised of the plot, wisely placed the conspirators under surveillance, and finally sentenced them to perpetual banishment from the country. Amongst the party there was a Catholic lady and two Jesuits. The latter, disguised as an apothecary and a physician's assistant, were met by Mr. Ellis on his return from Antananarivo. The so-called "assistant," however, proved to be the

Abbé Jouen, the principal of a Jesuit college at Bourbon. Such shameless pretenders were meet companions for reckless conspirators.

Had the frustration of the plot and the banishment of its authors been the sole results of its discovery, it would not have been noticed here. But, unhappily, while the guilty escaped, the innocent suffered. How far any of the Christians, groaning under cruel oppression, and expecting deliverance from the proposed change in the Government, were drawn into the snare, is not known. But it was sufficient for the Queen that such were still amongst her subjects, notwithstanding all her edicts, her punishments, and her threats. She resolved, therefore, that, whether guilty or not, they should suffer for that which strangers had devised, and of which the great multitude of them had not even heard. And now, like the sudden eruption of the long pent-up fires of a volcano, the wrath of the Queen once more burst forth with desolating fury.

The 3rd of July, 1857, was one of those awful days of doom of which the Christians of Antananarivo had seen but too many during the present reign. Early in the morning of that day, the announcement was made by the Queen's officers that a great kabary was to be held. What this foreboded they knew but too well: and they did not conceal their fears; for together with the royal summons, came the intelligence that they were hemmed in by soldiers stationed at every outlet of the city, so that escape was impossible. At the same time, officers broke into their houses, and forcibly drove them to the place of the great assembly.

"There was," said an eye-witness, "a general howling and wailing, a rushing and running through the streets, as if the town had been attacked by a hostile army." At length the appointed hour came. Thousands of people strongly guarded were crowded together within the great square of the city, many of them waiting with dread the announcement of the royal pleasure, and when all was in readiness, a Queen's messenger delivered, with a loud voice, the following message from his dreaded mistress:—That the Queen had long suspected that there were many Christians still amongst her people, and that, within the last few days, she had discovered that several thousands of them dwelt in and around her capital;—that every one knew how she hated this sect, and how strictly she had forbidden the practice of their religion;—that she should do her utmost to discover the guilty, and would punish them with the greatest severity; and that all should die who did not, within fifteen days, submit themselves to her pleasure.

What added to the danger of the Christians was the circumstance that one of their worst foes had in his possession a list of the names of those who resided in the city. This was intended for the use of the Queen, and the dangerous document had actually been entrusted for delivery to one of her attendants. Providentially, this man was a firm friend of the Prince, and favourable to the Christians. He therefore brought the list to him. Rakoto read it, but the next moment it was torn into fragments and scattered upon the ground. This bold but prudent act saved many lives; and as the accused were now warned, numbers of them, as soon as they could find an egress from the city, either fled to the forest, or by other means escaped the fury of the storm. But all were not so fortunate. Some were seized and put to the torture to force them to disclose the names of their brethren; and while this was going on, soldiers searched the houses, and consigned every person suspected of Christianity to prison. One of the prisons used on that occasion had originally been a chapel, and to that sacred purpose it has now been restored by Radama II. But at the time of which we write, many Christians were crowded there and cruelly tormented, by a royal order. The name of the place where this prison-house stands, is AMBALINAKANGA. "It has," writes Mr. Ellis, "been the scene of much hope and disappointment, suffering and joy. Here the first Christian Church was formed, and the communion celebrated in May, 1831, when the natives of Madagascar first united with the Missionaries in commemorating the dying love of Christ. After the persecution broke out in 1836, the house of prayer was turned into a prison, in which, mingled with wretched criminals, the Christians were confined. This chapel was a prison when I was here in 1856. King Radama, since his accession, has restored it to its original use, and a most attentive congregation of about eight hundred people occupy it every Lord's-day. The people have almost as strong an attachment to this scene of their distress and sorrow, as to the spots on which their companions actually died." Here it is proposed to erect one of the memorial churches. Mr. Ellis states that "the site is admirable, being in the midst of a large population on a sort of rocky terrace, with building materials at hand."

What a contrast the scenes then witnessed, the sufferings then endured, and the dangers then impending present to the congregations who now, under the same roof, listen to God's Word, and with the voice of joy and melody, sing forth the honour of His name! Associated as it is with scenes so sorrowful and services so sacred, the strong attachment of the Christians to this spot is easily explained.

Six days after the promulgation of her decree, the Queen heard that comparatively few Christians had been apprehended. This made her more furious than before. Her insane rage indeed seemed to know no bounds. "The bowels of the earth," she said, "shall be searched, and the rivers and lakes shall be dragged with nets, rather than that one Christian shall escape." At the same time she issued new orders to the officers and soldiers of her army to track the Christians to their hiding-places; and another kabary was held, when it was proclaimed that whoever helped, or did not hinder their escape, should surely die. But these measures were to a large extent in vain, and, in some instances, the Queen's violence frustrated her design. In one village, nine miles from the capital, the entire population, thus forewarned, happily saved themselves by flight. Hoping to surprise the place and secure the victims, the Queen despatched fifteen hundred soldiers; but they came too late; the houses were empty, and the people safe.

The first victim of this cruel outburst of the enraged despot was an aged Christian female, who, before the nine days given for self-accusation, was dragged away to the market-place, and horrible to relate, her backbone was sawn asunder. This was on the 11th of July; but the next morning, six more Christians were taken at a village not far from the city. Their concealment, however, had been so contrived as very nearly to have prevented their discovery; for the soldiers had searched the hut in which they were hid, and were upon the point of leaving it, when one of them thought that he heard a cough. They therefore renewed their search, and soon, beneath some straw, they discovered a large hole, in which the hunted Christians were buried. Instantly and violently they were dragged out, bound, and hurried away to their doom. Nor, unhappily, did the consequences of this discovery end with them. It was evident that the other villagers had been privy to the concealment of their neighbours, and had generously kept the secret, even at the risk of their lives. Whether they themselves or any of them were believers in the Gospel is not known; but whatever might have been its cause, their kindness met with a sad requital. The commanding officer, who was a stern man, at once ordered his soldiers to seize them all, to bind them, and to lead them away with the six Christians whom they had sought to save to be punished.

It was said by those who saw her, that the Queen had never before given way to such outbursts of rage as now; and that at no former period had her purpose to exterminate the Christians been so fixed and furious. In the city, and the surrounding villages, kabaries were held almost daily for the purpose of denouncing them as the cause of all the evils which afflicted the land, and of declaring the Queen's determination not to rest until the last of this hated sect had been rooted out and destroyed; and had not the register of their names fallen into the hands of the Prince, there is too much reason to fear that his mother's sanguinary desires would have been largely gratified. But this was not the only aid which the watchful kindness of their friend and protector, together with the secret but earnest efforts of some Christian nobles who acted with him, now rendered to the oppressed. The liberation of many who had been apprehended must be attributed to them, amongst whom may be numbered several of the villagers who had connived at the concealment of their Christian neighbours. The marvel and the great mercy was that the Prince himself escaped; but his savage mother seemed dead to every human feeling save one—the love of her son. This instinct was the instrument which God used for the preservation of Radama's own life, and through him of the lives of His servants.

"And in respect to those who are in concealment, writes the native Christians, "and those who are in bonds, it is Rakoto and Ramonja who have taken on themselves the charge of concealing and protecting them, and giving them their daily bread. And those of his companions who have any property, give for this according to their ability. And those of their brethren who are in distress or want, though not in bonds or concealment, are looked after and cared for by these two princes, sometimes receiving from them clothes, rice, and even money. We know that such liberality presses hard at times upon their means, but they cannot abandon their own afflicted brethren, *for they are to them as their own flesh.*"

This princely succour was extended to the suffering Christians to the last. So late as June, 1861, some of those residing at the capital thus wrote to Mr. Ellis, "With respect to the royal prince, indeed, dear Sir, it causes us to rejoice and bless God that He supports, and makes the people of God strong to bear the affliction and trouble in Madagascar. Yet what he has done, he has done by the help of God, and we therefore bless the Most High on that account (Matt. xvi. 17), and not towards the Christians alone does he show kindness, but to the people in general, when he can. And when any evil or calamity overtakes a man, he prevents his being reported, if he can do it."

But notwithstanding these interpositions, human and Divine, not a few were at this period added to the number of Christian martyrs. Only fifteen days after the great kabary, ten were publicly executed, and their death was accompanied with frightful tortures. On their way to the place of execution, the soldiers goaded them along with their spears, and the blood-stained path through which they had been driven showed with what effect the weapons had been used. For what special reason is unknown, but it was ordered that they and others, to the number of twenty-one, should not suffer in any of the ordinary modes of execution. It is probable, however, that as the previous martyrdom of Christians had failed to accomplish the object of their persecutors, the Queen resolved to try the effect of a more painful method. They were therefore sentenced to be stoned, but not to death ; for ere life was extinct, or consciousness lost, their heads were to be severed from their mutilated bodies, and held up to the view of the multitude. But the Spirit which sustained Stephen, and so many of their brethren who had laid down their lives for the sake of the Lord Jesus, characterized these noble sufferers. Theirs was the same unwavering faith, the same patient suffering, the same victorious death. No faltering, no timid clinging to life, no compromise with conviction, cast the faintest shadow upon the worthy name they bore, or the holy cause for which they died. As they were led out from the prison to Fiaduna, amongst the sounds which first caught the ear was the voice of praise; and still, as they approached the fatal spot, notwithstanding the piercing of the spears, and even when crushed beneath the stones, they were happy, and almost jubilant. To quote the brief, but expressive words of a native witness of the scene, " They continued to sing hymns till they died."

Other details of this last dire persecution are still wanting; but it is known that the twenty-one who were stoned did not include all the martyrs of 1857. The Bishop of Mauritius thus refers to some who, at the same time, suffered at Arapimarinana. "We afterwards paid a visit to the four places in which the Christian martyrs had been sacrificed. These holy men* are resuming the labours of the Madagascar Mission under painfully interesting circumstances. The bones of some of the martyrs still remain where they fell; but Mr. Ellis did not wish to remove them for Christian burial until the Missionaries should arrive, and in this I fully concurred. Let Mr. Ellis say what was the effect produced upon him, and upon the Malagasy Christians, by the sight of this spectacle. We passed by spots where their bleached remains still lay ever since 1858 (1857), the martyrs having been precipitated down a height of at least seventy perpendicular feet. There striking against projecting rocks, they had rolled down a further descent of at least fifty feet. Those surviving relatives or friends who had been able to obtain the permission so to do had removed some of these melancholy remains, but the bodies of several of the martyrs, on being hurled from the precipice had been arrested in their descent by the wide-spreading branches of beech trees, planted there by English Missionaries many years previously; and evidences still exist of this fearful termination of their lingering agonies, and of the impossibility of according to them the last token of respect claimed by our common humanity." How many were hurled over the precipice of Arapimarinana in 1857, we have yet to learn, but it is certain that this was the most fatal of all the persecutions endured by the Christians of Madagascar, and that this large and honoured band most

* The six Missionaries sent out by the London Missionary Society, and now labouring at Antananarivo.

worthily closed the long line of faithful martyrs, who through much tribulation had preceded them to the kingdom of God.

It has been computed that rather more than a hundred suffered death in maintaining their Christian faith and fidelity during the late Queen's reign; and although this computation cannot be exactly verified in the present incomplete state of our information, enough is certainly known to warrant the assumption that this is at least a very near approximation to the truth. But while so many thus endured a violent death by the hand of the public executioner, a far larger number perished, some of them miserably, by the tangena, in heavy chains, in servile labour, in the pestilential prison, in forest, and mountain, and dens, and caves of the earth, to which they had fled from their implacable foes. Thus, at the period to which we have just referred, between fifty and sixty were compelled to drink the tangena, eight of whom died, while nearly sixty were manacled, and a still larger number reduced to slavery, many of whom subsequently followed their martyred brethren to their rest and reward. "These all died in faith." "They overcome by the blood of the Lamb and the word of His testimony." "Therefore are they before the throne of God."

From the letter of June, 1861, already quoted, we cite another passage to show the state of the country and of the Christians almost up to the day when the shadow of death was suddenly turned into morning. "The distress of the people here is increasing daily; for they are in darkness, and have no knowledge. The country is not tranquil. * * Let us ask the God of mercy that darkness may be scattered from the land of Madagascar. * * Pray, dear Sir, that the blessing of Jesus Christ may be with us and with you, and that we may be helped to receive the exhortation given by you to us, and to endure the affliction that is so severe. May we have love and courage during our lifetime upon earth (Rom. v. 8—11.), and may the God of Peace quickly subdue the work of Satan, and advance the knowledge of the people respecting Jesus Christ (2 Cor. ix. 10; x. 15)."

But the day was at hand, and happily we have now written the closing record of the wrongs and sufferings of the faithful and much enduring Christians of Madagascar. Deliverance was almost immediately to follow the persecution last described. The cry from beneath the altar had been heard; the rod of the oppressor was broken, and a future full of high and holy promise then opened to invite the servants of God to consecrate their works of faith and their labours of love, to the evangelization of that noble land. The prominent features of this great revolution we must now briefly sketch.

Ranavalona, the Queen of Madagascar, was of advanced age; and her reign had extended to thirty-three years. But the day of her death drew near. For several weeks during the summer of 1861 her strength rapidly failed, and her symptoms appeared so dangerous, that early in August it was generally known that the sceptre would speedily pass into other hands. But by whom would it be swayed? This was *the* question with the people, and it was asked earnestly and anxiously by tens of thousands. Had the decision rested with them, the issue would not have been doubtful; their choice, cordial and almost unanimous, would have been Rakoto-radama. Long had their hope and their desire been fixed upon him, for no other man in Madagascar was so honoured, trusted, and beloved. During many years he had stood between the oppressor and the oppressed, and in instances without number, in opposition to his mother's strongest and sternest mandates, and at the peril of his own life, he had rescued the victims of her wrath from chains, from slavery, and from death. Long had the interests of his country and the highest welfare of its inhabitants been the object of his intense solicitude; but, while the benefactor of all classes, he had been the especial friend and protector of the Christians.

"I hear continually," writes Mr. Ellis, "of the great clemency of the King, and am not surprised at the affectionate feelings with which he is regarded by the people. I have been told by an officer who knows him well, that, while *Prince* of Madagascar, he used to be deeply affected at the suffering and misery inflicted on the people, and the false promises by which they were often ensnared to their ruin. Some officers, his most particular friends, have told me of many of his attempts to mitigate the severities of the late Government. They stated that when they first united themselves with him he said, 'Our great object must be to lessen the sufferings of the people, to prevent unjust accusations, and undeserved and excessive punishments; to rescue, if possible, those sentenced to death, and to do all we can to save the lives of the people. God will help us, for it is right to do it, and God will protect us.' In carrying out these purposes of justice and benevolence, they had often been in great danger, but had never been apprehended. The Prince said also, 'We must study the customs, the feelings, and the habits of the people, that, while we try to do good, we may not be entrapped, and put to death. We must not make any boast or stir about what we are doing; let the people find out what our motives are by our doings. We must always do good—all kinds of good.' These officers said that, by night and day, in darkness, storm, and rain, the Prince would be with them, sharing all their dangers, never deterred by any difficulty from either going to the high authorities and pleading for the prisoners and the oppressed, or to favour the escape of others who were sentenced to death. His great wish was that the people should be free, enlightened and prosperous. He had, therefore, on his accession to the throne, recalled all from banishment, abrogated all cruel laws, given liberty of conscience to all, set free all the prisoners taken in war, and sent them home with presents."

The following instances illustrate these features of the Prince's character. One morning while at breakfast with his friends, a woman in tears entered the room and casting herself at his feet, told him that many people in her village had been condemned to die, amongst whom were her husband and children, and prayed that he would save their lives. Instantly he ordered some of his attendants to go and deliver the poor people from their terrible fate. They hastened to the spot, but soon returned to say that the prison was surrounded by so many soldiers that it was impossible for them to get near it. On hearing this, the Prince mounted his horse, and rode with haste to the village. As soon as he reached it, he proceeded to the prison, spoke to the guards in an authoritative tone, seized the sword of the officer in command, forced his way to the condemned persons, broke their chains, and told them to make their escape. Then, turning to the officer, who stood silent and astonished at the rapidity and boldness of this movement, the Prince said to him, "Should any one inquire who has done this, tell him that it was the son of the Queen; but do not name it until the prisoners are out of reach."

At another time, he was informed that the inhabitants of a Christian village were to be denounced to the Queen; but having ascertained who was to be their accuser, he sent for her, and by the wise and firm measures he employed, saved the people from the threatened danger.

It was not surprising, therefore, that his accession to the throne should have been regarded with bright hopes and eager desire. But pitfalls and perils had for years beset his path. Though beloved by the people generally, his identification with the Christians made him many foes, who had repeatedly sought his life. On one occasion, seven men, armed with knives and spears, laid wait for him in the road along which it was known that he would travel, and it was only by spurring his horse and rushing in amongst the band of assassins that he escaped. But a danger now awaited him greater than most of those from which he had been delivered.

The Prince had a rival in his cousin Rambosalama, the son of the Queen's sister, and brother of his own wife. This man the Queen had nominated at the commencement of her reign as her successor; but when the unexpected birth of a son gave a rightful heir to the throne of the Hovas, Rambosalama lost his title. Nevertheless, he resolved, if possible, to secure the object of his ambition. Nor was he without the hope of success. Resolute, contriving, and unscrupulous, he had gained over to his side the Queen's chief adviser, Rainijoary, and many who stood near the throne; while with herself, whom he too closely resembled in his hatred of the Christians, he was a great favourite. It was confidently reported, and commonly believed, that Rambosalama had hired assassins to remove his only obstacle in the path to power, and that more than once these wretched men had confessed to the Prince their meditated crime. Be this as it may, it is certain that Rakoto and his friends well knew the purpose, and probably the plots of his rival. Amongst those upon whom he placed his chief reliance, was his long-tried Christian associate, the commander of the forces. This man, who had attained the highest honour (the 15th) which the Queen could confer, and more absolute power, as the head of the army, than any other of her subjects, was, as our readers may remember, the son of Rainiharo, so long prime minister, and the bitter persecutor of the Christians. The second officer in command was also one of the Prince's warm supporters. Nevertheless, it required the utmost vigilance and skill to frustrate the purpose of Rambosalama and his co-conspirators.

About a month before the Queen's death, the Prince and his friends agreed that the time had come when it behoved them to adopt measures for their own protection. In most cases, we know what those measures would have been,—the chain, the dungeon, and the dagger. But Rakoto, always remarkable for his humanity, had resolved not to pass to power over the fallen and the dead. His sole purpose was to preserve, not to punish—to save his own life, not to sacrifice that of others; and all his plans at this period were governed by this purpose. But to prevent surprise, and to be fully prepared for the coming change, he and his advisers often met in council. Hence, when the necessity arose they were ready to act with concord, promptitude, and decision.

Aware of his cousin's proceedings, Rambosalama at this time showed signs of great distrust, and moved about as if expecting an attack from some secret foe. He seldom left his house, and never entered the palace without being armed himself, and accompanied by armed followers. When the commander-in-chief heard of this, he issued an order that no armed person should enter the royal residence, and that the utmost vigilance should be used in the execution of this command. To show that it would be impartially applied, the Prince and himself were the first who submitted to be searched. Of course Rambosalama and his confederates could do no less without an open declaration of their traitorous design. It was at this time that Rakoto said to his cousin, "Lay aside your arms; trust me, they might be turned against you."

Another precaution employed was to conceal the orders, which from day to day regulated the movements of the soldiers, from all in whom the Prince and the commander-in-chief had not confidence. Amongst others this knowledge was withheld from Rainijoary. This opened the eyes of the crafty and cruel old councillor, who, abandoning the hope of seeing Rambosalama on the throne, now deemed it prudent to make terms with the Prince. He therefore deserted his former associates, and promised to submit to Rakoto as the Queen's successor.

At length, at dawn of day on the 16th of August, the intelligence spread through the city that the Queen was stricken with death, and that in a few hours all would be over. Soon an immense crowd filled every avenue to the palace, and was even pressing within the courts. For what purpose were they come? Had you marked the features of some of them, watched their secret and suspicious movements, and noticed the deadly weapons which they vainly attempted to conceal, their design would have been but too plainly disclosed. These were the partizans of Rambosalama; they had been brought there, that, at a given signal from him, they might cut his pathway to the vacant throne. But while the son was weeping at the death-bed of his mother, the faithful commander of the forces had his keen eye fixed full upon every movement of her would-be successor. He knew his plans and his partizans; watched his movements within the palace, and followed him from the chamber of death, as he hastened to give the concerted signal to his ready instruments, who were waiting without. But on his way, and ere he could effect his purpose, he was seized, and hurried back in safe custody. Almost at the same instant a trumpet sounded, and more than a thousand soldiers, who were awaiting this summons, marched in strong array, and with quickened steps, to the palace.

Rakoto was now safe: his foes had been foiled, and his rival a prisoner. Soon the commander-in-chief appeared upon the balcony of the palace to announce the Queen's death, and to proclaim Radama II. King of Madagascar. In a moment, loud shouts and wild demonstrations of joy broke forth from the soldiers and multitude, which soon spread through the capital. For a time the people seemed intoxicated with delight, and when, towards the afternoon of the day, it was rumoured that Radama would present himself to his subjects, every approach to the palace was again thronged. About four o'clock, arrayed in the robes of royalty, with the crown upon his head, and surrounded by his chief nobles, the King appeared. It was long ere the shouts and cries of the people could be hushed; but as soon as silence was obtained, in a few expressive words he begged them to be calm, and then assured them (and never, we believe, were words more truthful) that, in becoming their sovereign, his one desire was to devote himself to their welfare, and to that of the country over which he reigned.

Meanwhile, Rambosalama was conducted under a strong guard to the centre of the city, to the lake Andohalo, where he was compelled to take the oath of allegiance to his cousin: After this, he was conveyed to a residence of his own in the country, there to be detained a prisoner, under a guard of two hundred soldiers. But this was the extent of his punishment. Not a fetter bound his limbs, not a fraction of his large wealth was forfeited, nor was he forbidden to communicate with his friends. Such was the generosity, the magnanimity—we cannot term it justice— with which the King treated the man who had conspired against his title and his life.

The revolution thus brought about soon made itself felt. "The sun," writes Mr. Ellis, "did not set on the day on which Radama II. became King of Madagascar before he had proclaimed equal protection to all its inhabitants, and declared that every man was free to worship God according to the dictates of his own conscience, without fear or danger. He sent his officers to open the prison doors, to knock off the fetters from those to whom the joyous shouts of the multitude without had already announced that the day of their deliverance was come. He despatched others to recall the remnant of the condemned ones from the remote and pestilential districts to which they had been banished, and where numbers had died from disease, or exhaustion from the rude and heavy bars of iron with which they had been chained from neck to neck together. The exiles hastened home; men and women, worn and wasted with suffering and want, reappeared in the city, to the astonishment of their neighbours—who had deemed them long since dead—but to the grateful joy of their friends. The long-desired jubilee had come, and gladness and rejoicing everywhere prevailed; for many who were not believers in the Gospel, sympathized with the Christians in their sufferings, and rejoiced in their deliverance."

Seven of these restored exiles thus speak of themselves and others: "On Thursday, 29th of August, 1861, we that were in concealment appeared. Then all the people were astonished, when they saw us, that we were alive, and not yet buried or eaten by the dogs; and there were a great many of the people desiring to see us, for they considered us as dead; and this is what astonished them. On the 9th of September, those that were in fetters came to Antananarivo; but they could not walk, on account of the weight of their heavy fetters, and their weak and feeble bodies."

To pass over other proceedings which show how much the King desired the social and political prosperity of the country, one of his earliest acts was to lay the foundation of a large stone building as a college, and to restore the schools throughout the country which had been closed by his mother. This was a suitable and most significant commencement of his reign, and gave a pledge to the people that he designed to act out all his previous patriotic professions. It is obviously the high ambition of Radama II. to sway the sceptre over an enlightened, peaceful, and happy people; to rule, not by the sword, but by the press, the pulpit, and the school, by truth, justice, and liberty. The first Radama was undoubtedly a remarkable man, considering the circumstances in which he was placed. But he was selfish, despotic, ambitious, and cruel. He delighted in war, and was regardless of all rights which impeded the extension of his dominions. Even his suppression of the slave trade, the favour he showed to education, and his tolerance of Missionary efforts were clearly traceable to very inferior motives. But in all these respects the contrast between him and the reigning monarch is very marked. "When," writes Mr. Ellis, "during a conversation we had lately in presence of the Queen and others, some comparisons were drawn between the compassion of Queen Victoria towards the poor and afflicted, and his own kindness towards the persecuted Christians, the King looked at me, as if for my approval. I said he had, in many respects, 'all that could be desired by a people in their King.' He looked grave, and said, 'Mr. Ellis knows what is in my heart; he knows that I desire to know and serve God. I pray to God to enlighten my mind, and teach me what is right, and what I ought to know and do.' The company appeared all very much interested in these remarks."

Such a desire as Radama II. thus expressed may account for what he has already done, and should produce strong confidence in his future government. And it is most remarkable that he should have formed views of policy so large and liberal, so enlightened, humane, and patriotic as those which form the foundation of his throne;—that the son of such a mother, trained up under a despotism so dark, and restrictive and cruel, should have adopted such principles of religious freedom and political economy, as equal civil liberty and universal free trade principles, which our own nation has been so slow to learn, and which are still repudiated in many lands where civilization is far advanced, and a form of Christianity professed. The case is without a parallel. And while, perhaps, considering his past identification with the Christians, we may not be as much surprised that he should favour education and Missionary labours, his conduct in this respect, even more if possible than the general and generous principles of his government, assures us that, should his life be spared, he will in God's hands be a mighty instrument in raising Madagascar to a new and noble position amongst civilized and Christian communities.

While Radama II. was thus showing that God had given to him what He gave to Solomon, "largeness of heart," the Christians improved their new-found privileges. No longer gathering together by stealth in secret places, or at the midnight hour, they now met in the very heart of the city, in buildings which their own sovereign had set apart for Divine service, and in the broad face of day; while "their unquenchable thirst after instruction," their "industry in acquiring knowledge," "the vitality and strength of the faith by which they have been sustained," "their activity and force of character," "their clear perceptions of the saving truths of the Gospel," "their family religion," their "large congregations in the city," and "the smaller assemblies in almost every village in the surrounding country," together with "the great influence for good which the sufferers of Christ exercise over their brethren by the simple, humble recital of their sufferings, always given with devout acknowledgment and thanks for the Divine consolation they received, may well encourage the most sanguine hopes for the future." *

Together with the intelligence of the Queen's death, letters reached this country which made it plain to the Directors of the London Missionary Society that Missionaries, so long excluded from Madagascar, would now receive, both from the King and from the people, a cordial welcome. Six weeks after the Queen's death four of the pastors in the capital thus wrote:—"We are filled with joy that the kingdom of God gains ground, and establishes itself more and more in our country. We have begun to meet for public worship at Antananarivo since Lord's-day, 29th September last. As one house was not large enough to contain us all, we had to meet in eleven separate houses, and they were all crowded to excess. When the people saw how great was the number of Christians, they were exceedingly amazed; and what increased their astonishment was the appearing in public of Christians who, having been hidden for so long a period, were considered by all as dead. Everybody could not but exclaim, 'Truly, God is great, who can thus watch over those who place their confidence in Him!' A general disposition to join us seems to take

* Letter from Rev. W. Ellis.

hold of the people. * * The King, Radama II., tells us to write, and persuade the Missionaries to come and settle at Antananarivo, as well as our friends and countrymen who are at Mauritius. There is now no obstacle; the way is open to everybody."

To the London Missionary Society belongs the great privilege and honour of being not only the first, but the only Protestant Society whose agents have laboured in Madagascar. The Embassy sent by the British Government to congratulate Radama II. on his accession to the throne, when referring to the cordiality with which Englishmen were welcomed to the capital, truly remark in their official report of the visit, "We need not look far for an explanation of this feeling. The Missionary work, initiated thirty* years ago, will sufficiently account for it. Nearly all the arts with which the people were acquainted, were taught them by the Missionaries."

It may be easily believed that the intelligence that Madagascar was at length open to Christian Missionaries, and that the King was prepared to welcome them to his country, filled the hearts of the Directors of the London Missionary Society, and of many other Christians throughout the country, with devout gratitude and gladness. Long and anxiously had they waited, and fervently had they prayed for the period which had now arrived. Impelled, therefore, by every Christian feeling and conviction, they immediately addressed themselves to the

---

* It should have been "forty."

sacred task of re-occupying the field where their agents had so successfully laboured, where so much had been suffered for Christ, and which since then had so strongly called forth their sympathy, solicitude, and supplications.

The King of Madagascar was well aware that it was their purpose to do this at the earliest practical period. He therefore, immediately after ascending the throne, instructed his principal Secretary of State to invite the Rev. J. Le Brun, the Society's Missionary at Mauritius, to visit the capital without delay. Too aged to undertake the toilsome journey, Mr. Le Brun deputed his son—accompanied by David Johns, long an evangelist to his countrymen in the Mauritius—to undertake the service. As soon as this intelligence reached the Directors, they began preparations for the resumption of the Mission. But while these were in progress, on the 20th of November, 1861, at their earnest request, Mr. Ellis sailed on his fourth visit to Madagascar; and on the 15th of April, 1862, he was followed by six Missionaries, including a doctor of medicine, a superintendent of schools, and a printer.

Since the departure of those brethren, almost every mail has brought the Directors such reports from Madagascar, as have filled their hearts with wonder, joy, and thankfulness. From Mr. Le Brun they learned that, before reaching Antananarivo, he received a letter of welcome in the King's name, announcing that His Majesty had appropriated a house for his use, and had sent officers to conduct him to it. The day after his arrival was the Sabbath, but it was not to him a season of rest. At an early hour his house was invaded by Christian friends, and from nine o'clock until two he was led from one congregation to another, that he might, though in an unknown tongue and by an interpreter, utter some words of prayer to God, and exhortation to the people. During that Sabbath morning he took part in the services at five sanctuaries. "Wherever I went," he writes, "I was saluted with tears and expressions of joy; and whenever I pronounced the blessed name of Jesus Christ, it was truly affecting to witness the utterance of deep emotion by which they testified their faith and gratitude."

Mr. Le Brun's brief but active engagements in the capital were terminated by illness shortly after his arrival there. But this visit elicited many demonstrations of affection on the part of the Christians. "Day after day, night after night," he writes, "it was the same loving care, mingled with prayer and supplication. Oh, how fervently did they pray as they knelt by the side of my couch! What tears of fraternal love and Christian sympathy they shed, as they administered medicines, and watched with anxiety their effect upon me!"

But though his opportunities of observation and intercourse were thus restricted, Mr. Le Brun had a most cheering audience of the King, a solemn conference with the pastors, thrilling recitals of danger and deliverance from the lips of returned exiles, and proofs, which filled him with amazement, of the large number and rapid increase of believers. As soon as he had strength for the journey he left that place, with his spirit greatly refreshed and strengthened by all that he had seen and heard there of the power and progress of the Gospel.

On the arrival of the healthy season, Mr. Ellis sailed for Tamatave, where he arrived towards the end of May. As he stepped on shore, an officer of the palace, who had been specially sent by the King for the purpose, welcomed him to Madagascar in his royal master's name, and stated that he had been appointed to escort him to the capital. The officer then handed to Mr. Ellis a letter from Radama II., in which the King expressed his desire to see him. The same letter informed him of the death of Rambosalama, thus dissipating the fear which he had reasonably felt for the safety of Radama. After this cordial reception, Mr. Ellis was conducted by a procession of chiefs and officers to the King's house, which a number of native workmen had for some days been preparing for his temporary residence. As soon as he entered, he was formally presented with the house. The next morning, however, he accepted an invitation to sojourn with the chief judge of Tamatave, where he was honoured with many presents, and treated with the utmost kindness and consideration.

On the following day, the Christians held a thanksgiving service, at which " a goodly number was present," and "many seemed deeply moved." "Their prayers," writes Mr. Ellis, "were appropriate, earnest, and simple, their singing earnest and apparently sincere, the reading of the Scriptures very impressive, and the comments plain and pointed. You cannot imagine the sensation my

K

arrival has occasioned, and the satisfaction I derive from all I see and hear about the Christians."

After Mr. Ellis had spent a week at Tamatave, a special messenger from the King arrived to hasten his departure for the capital. Accordingly, he left early the next morning (May 31), and on the 16th of June he reached his destination. When within thirty miles of Antananarivo, he was met by a large number of Christians from that city, headed by two of their pastors; but instead of expressing their joy by ordinary salutations, they came towards him with the voice of thanksgiving and melody. No reception could have been more cordial or more touching; and tears, he tells us, were the only response he could make to the devout gladness of his friends. This real *Te Deum* ended, the pastors announced that they had been sent by their brethren and the Churches to bid him welcome, to assure him of their delight, and to accompany him to the capital.

Ten miles further on they rested for the Sabbath-day, at a village called Ambotomanga. Here seven officers of high rank, who had been sent by the King, met him and attended worship, in which they joined with much apparent earnestness. This was a high day to Mr. Ellis. As he saw the chief room of the largest house in the place " thronged with simple and devout worshippers, while numbers crowded around on the outside," he was much affected while reflecting upon the change thus indicated in the circumstances of the Christians since his former visit in 1854. Then, when tarrying for a Sabbath in the same place, only a few dared to meet him for prayer, and they came by stealth and at night; but now not only was the room filled, but numbers crowded round on the outside.

Next morning, letters of welcome from the King and the principal Secretary of State were put into his hands, and soon after nine o'clock, the party, consisting of about two hundred persons, set out for the capital. As they approached the city, and all along the suburbs, the gathered multitudes gave him a warm reception. On the following day he was most cordially received by the King and Queen at the palace, in the presence of the nobles of the Court, who expressed their great gratification at the expression of friendship on the part of the English, and the endeavours of the London Missionary Society to impart to his people the blessings of Christianity and education. "The prime minister," writes Mr. Ellis, "the commander-in-chief, the first officer of the palace, and other high authorities, some of them apparently most earnest Christians, were equally cordial in their welcomes and in their conferences with me at their own residences, in which I have been their guest."

During the next week, Mr. Ellis's house was thronged with Christian friends, not merely with those who resided in the capital, but with others from distant parts of the country. The only drawback to his joy in meeting them was the disappointment which many evinced when told that he had not been able to bring with him—what they longed to possess—copies of God's Word. Nor was this disappointment surprising, as some entire congregations did not possess a single copy. Nevertheless, Mr. Ellis found "their faith simple, scriptural, and firm; with no deviation in their teaching or belief from the great essential truths of the Gospel; no visionary or erratic opinions on the subject of religion, which seems to be with them a simple, sincere, earnest, personal concern."

On the two following Sabbaths, Mr. Ellis attended two of their places of worship, which consisted of houses with the partitions and fronts removed to afford sufficient accommodation. Each of these rude sanctuaries, with an intermission of two hours, was densely filled from daybreak to five o'clock with congregations of about fifteen hundred persons. "No description," Mr. Ellis writes, "can convey to you any correct idea of the seriousness, attention, apparent devotion, and deep feeling of these assemblies during the time of worship."

We cannot, and indeed need not follow Mr. Ellis through the details of his almost incessant occupations. The subjoined extracts will sufficiently show their number, interest, and importance.

"I am occasionally sent for by the King or some of the high officers, and I have for some short time past attended His Majesty at his house daily, from one to three o'clock, to read English with him. We read together out of a large quarto Bible, on the outside of which is inscribed in gilt letters, 'Presented to Radama, King of Madagascar, by the London Missionary Society, 1821.' A number of officers, some of them Christians, are generally present, and we frequently converse on what we have read. I have also every forenoon at my house eleven or twelve sons of the chief nobles and officers, who come to learn English an hour and a half daily. They will be the future rulers of the country. They accompany me to the chapel, and sometimes to my readings with the King. Last Sunday, with His Majesty's approval, I held Divine service at the King's house at three o'clock in the afternoon; His Majesty, some of his high officers, all my pupils, and a number of others, were present. I read in the Old and New Testament; we sang twice; when I prayed, partly in English, and partly in Malagasy, concluding with the Lord's Prayer in Malagasy. Then I occupied about a quarter of an hour in an address from 1 Tim. i. 15: 'This is a faithful saying, and worthy of all acceptation, that Christ Jesus came into the world to save sinners.' This was faithfully translated by Ra Haniraka. All were very attentive. I was informed that the King expressed his approval, and I hope to be permitted to continue the service. I have seen nothing yet to diminish the high opinion I had formed of the strength and purity of the religious feeling among the people. I attend the King daily, read the Scriptures with him, and converse with him on their contents as well as on other matters. I continue my Sunday service at his house, and, as I am told by his officers, with increasing interest and satisfaction to the King, who sometimes interrupts me to express his entire concurrence in something I may have said, or to impress it more forcibly upon the minds of the hearers. Besides these engagements—which take the best hours of every day, viz., from half-past ten in the morning till three in the afternoon—my house, during other intervals, is seldom free from persons who come to seek medical aid, or instruction and advice on religious subjects."

In further illustration of the public services of the Christians, of their devout habits, and of the position and prospects of Christianity in Madagascar, the following extracts from an address which the Bishop of Mauritius, who in July followed Mr. Ellis to Antananarivo, delivered at the Annual Meeting of the Mauritius Auxiliary Missionary Society, held at Port Louis, on the 30th of September, 1862, are no less important than interesting.

"The Resolution," said the Bishop, "alludes to the 'silent extension of Christian truth in Madagascar,' 'and the signal demonstration of the Divine blessing upon the reading of the Word of God.' I think I may say with truth that I was never more impressed in my life with anything, than I was at witnessing the results occasioned by the spread of Christian truth in Madagascar! It is my firm opinion that it is impossible for any one to feel the full force of this impression unless he has witnessed and studied it himself. The effect of Christian teaching in Madagascar struck me as possessing a most remarkable character. And it was introduced to my mind in this manner :—I was requested to attend a meeting of some of the natives. I said that I would do so if I could; but the heat of the season was so great that I could not remain on shore, and was compelled to go back to the ship. I there received a letter, addressed to me as 'The Bishop of Mauritius, our beloved brother on board the ship,' expressive of the Christians' regret at my inability to be amongst them on the occasion to which I had been invited, and requesting me to attend in the evening. In compliance with the request just alluded to, I went on shore in the evening, and found more than a hundred persons met together to receive me. They listened most attentively to the Word of God; and their praying and singing were of the most fervent character. They expressed great pleasure at seeing me, and intimated their earnest desire to have Christian teachers sent amongst them. After leaving Tamatave and proceeding towards the capital, the road lies on the right hand, the sea being on the left. Four attendants left the port with me, and three of these remained with me until I arrived at the capital, one having left me on the way. They were ever ready to enter upon the exercise of prayer. As an instance, I may mention that on one evening I was obliged from fatigue to go into my cot, and fell asleep. I was awakened in the early morning by the voices of persons who were engaged in reading the Scriptures and in prayer, and on inquiry I was informed that these exercises had been carried on throughout the night. They were ever ready for prayer and for reading the Scriptures—more so, indeed, than I was able at all times to assist in, owing to my being sick with fever. Proceeding along our journey, we came to a place called 'Indivaranty,' where we met with many Christians, who walked out through the village towards us, to welcome us. On arriving at the village we went to a house, where we found a woman who is the aunt of a man now in this room, and who was a listener to the Missionaries who were expelled nearly thirty years ago. The *honesty* of the people—in a part of the country where there is no police, and no magistrate or judge—particularly struck me. On one occasion I held a meeting, when three fine young men came in, whom I found to be Christians. They had each a copy of a Malagasy hymn book, and they 'started' the singing of well-known English sacred airs.

"In testimony of their desire to read and to hear the Word of God, I now hold in my hand a copy of the New Testament which when I left Mauritius was quite strong, and all but new. I was only a few weeks in Madagascar; but such was the desire of the people to handle the sacred volume, that my copy of it has been reduced to the state which frequent usage of it by them now exhibits it to you. All of these young men were able to read, and one of them engaged in prayer. This was precisely the state of things I met with throughout my passage from the coast to the capital. In the capital and in its immediate neighbourhood, I was struck by yet more sterling proofs of the abiding power of God's Word; for, in spite of the cruel persecutions of the late Queen, there are at this hour many thousands more of openly-pronounced Christians than there were known to be at the ejection of the Missionaries in 1845. I met with many Christians who appeared to have had the truth brought to their knowledge in a very special and striking manner. Some of these I particularly questioned. One of them had been taught Christianity by a Hova mother; she had been seized, imprisoned, and had almost miraculously escaped; seized again, she was again imprisoned, and put to death with horrible torture. With reference to the way in which the Bible has been circulated, and its knowledge spread abroad in Madagascar, I will only mention one further instance:—A young man possessed a Bible, which he had invariably carried about his person during a period of eighteen years. In the course of that long period of time, his Bible had frequently been exposed to the danger of destruction; but he had dwelt with peculiar confidence and satisfaction upon that passage which is found in Jer. xlvi. 27:—'But fear not thou, O my servant Jacob, and be not dismayed, O Israel: for behold, I will save thee from afar off, and thy seed from the land of their captivity; and Jacob shall return and be in rest and at ease, and none shall make him afraid.' That poor man had read this in the midst of his troubles, and he was not afraid. He went on in his way; 'and here,' he said to me, 'we are now, in good health and in safety.' He further quoted to me the 11th and 12th verses of the 42nd chapter of the book above cited:—'Be not afraid,' &c.: and six other similar passages from the Word of God.

"Mention is made, Sir, in the Resolution I hold in my hand, of the 'active and cruel opposition' which the Word of God has encountered in Madagascar. The proofs of this, which are still in existence, are most striking. I was shown a chain, although the person who showed it to me had previously stated that he 'did not like' to exhibit it. It consisted of very heavy iron rings—now broken and cut through—and had been for many years around the ankles of a poor Christian woman, whose life those rings had helped to wear away! Other instruments of torture —one of them a long iron bar with adjusting rings—were shown to me, by a person who bore marks of the sufferings they had occasioned, and must carry those marks to his grave; and, in spite of all this, the Word of God has yet gone on and prevailed.*

"In speaking of the second part of this Resolution, the resumption of Missionary enterprise in Madagascar—when I was there, I could not help being impressed with the feeling, that, had we attempted, one year ago, the Mission upon which we were then engaged, we every one of us ran the certain risk of being put to death!

"Arriving on the heights of Tananarivo, I never saw scenery more beautiful than was there spread out before me. In the dwelling occupied by the General and myself,

---

* Mr. Ellis informs us that he seldom preaches without seeing some of the Christians who have thus suffered amongst his hearers, and that occasionally, two or three come to his residence in the evening with their relatives, and with one of the native pastors, and remain for family worship. Amongst these are individuals who had long worn heavy fetters—fetters now happily struck off from their limbs, and on their way to the Missionary Museum in Blomfield Street. Another iron ring was worn by an eminent Christian woman, the wife of a native pastor, who died in her chains rather than deny the Lord who bought her. During the persecution, her husband was one of the most earnest and efficient preachers. But he was able to conceal himself until the storm was overpast, when he reappeared amongst his brethren, and has resumed the work to which God had called him. "The more," writes Mr. Ellis, "I see of these Christians, the more I admire and praise God for their patient endurance and humble triumph."

we overlooked the whole of the city. Mr. Ellis, who was present at one of the meetings held here, said there must have been at least 1500 persons present. I never saw anything like the fervour I there witnessed. I shortly afterwards again addressed the people, when from 1000 to 1400 persons were present—a mighty crowd pressing us in upon all sides. Whilst I addressed them a kind of electric feeling seemed to possess and pervade the whole assembly. I spoke to them of the fulness of the blessing of the Gospel of Christ. The Rev. Mr. Ellis interpreted my observations, and their effect so gratified me that I recalled those lines of Dr. Watts:—

> 'In holy duties let the day
> In holy pleasures pass away!'

"Mr. Ellis commences his services early, and concludes them at 11 A.M. To see the people swarm along the streets, produces much the effect of a swarm of bees around a beehive. My firm impression is, that it is not of the least use to attempt to spread the Roman Catholic religion in Madagascar. One of the Roman Catholic priesthood whom I met there, observed to me that one might just as well attempt to *cut a rock with a razor*, as attempt to make Roman Catholics of the Malagasy!

"Before leaving the capital for Tamatave, I asked Mr. Ellis if he was prepared to undertake the immediate responsibility of conducting the Mission. He unhesitatingly replied 'Yes.' He stated also that the whole coast was open; that Missionaries were on their way out; and that everything was ready for missionary labour, even to the very centre of Tananarivo. Some of the first and most influential young men in the island are studying under Mr. Ellis's instructions, and one of the highest officers in the army has learnt his alphabet under his care, almost in a single lesson; he had been regularly put through his lesson, and very speedily learnt it. On my way back from the capital, I met with the Missionaries of the London Missionary Society on their upward journey. I need not say that this meeting made us all exceedingly glad. They first joined in the services of our Liturgy, and we then held a service in the Malagasy language. * * *

"The King, anxious that his people should be relieved from the burdens which had borne so heavily upon them under the reign of the late Queen, has remitted all taxation. He is most anxious to insure for them the blessing of education, and is himself engaged in superintending the building of a large school-house in the capital, to which he accompanied me every day during my stay there. One of the Missionaries recently arrived was to take charge of this school on its completion. As we are now specially met to speak of the Bible, it may be as well to state what took place when we went up to the palace to present the copy of the Bible to the King, with which I was specially entrusted. The officers of the court, when I presented that Bible, received me amidst two rows of their ladies, all dressed in strange and almost barbaric splendour. The address I had written for the occasion was admirably translated by one of the high officers of the palace, and some of the sentences were so constructed as to be most suitable for Oriental literature.

"The King seemed to enter with much feeling into some portions of this address, and at its close shook me most cordially by the hand. This will illustrate the feelings he has regarding the sacred volume; and I trust it will quicken the sentiment of devotion with which we as Christians should implore the blessing upon him, and that, in the language of this Resolution, 'he may wear his crown with wisdom, and in peace and prosperity, until he obtains an incorruptible crown in the Kingdom of Heaven.'"

It has been already stated that Mr. Ellis visited Madagascar as the pioneer of the six Missionaries whom the Directors of the London Missionary Society had appointed to labour in the capital. But from the time of his arrival he was compelled to give himself to direct Missionary work, which, with numerous other heavy demands upon his time and strength, was all but overwhelming, and made him long for the day when his younger brethren should join him. It was, therefore, with great delight that, at the end of August, he heard that they were on their way up to the capital. This satisfaction was shared by many of all classes, but by no one more entirely than by Radama. "The King," writes Mr. Ellis, under date the 30th August, "sent off early in the morning four officers of the palace to welcome the Missionaries, and conduct them up to the capital. General Johnstone* called and

* The chief of the British Embassy, who was then awaiting the coronation, as representative of the British Government.

said he would go with me to meet them, and Captain Anson also went, to invite them to take refreshment at their quarters. The Christians were busily preparing their houses for them. These they had made look very comfortable, and had provided a most abundant supply of provisions. I went to the brow of the hill, and saw them in the distance. We descended, and at the bottom of the hill on which the city stands met and welcomed them—that is, the first detachment of their party, consisting of the two married couples and Mr. Stagg. I hastened to prepare them some tea and other refreshment, after which they appeared quite recruited, and pleased with their accommodation.

"I saw them again early on the following morning, the Sabbath, when all but Dr. Davidson, who had been ill, went with me to Analakely, where above a thousand persons were assembled for worship, whose countenances brightened as we entered. When I introduced the Missionaries to the King and Queen, they both expressed themselves much gratified by their safe arrival, and by the prospect of instruction and improvement to their people. They also expressed much pleasure at the arrival of English ladies, and more than once said, 'May God bless you, and preserve you in health and comfort here.' The General and the other English officers also publicly congratulated the Missionaries on their arrival.

"On the 4th of September I accompanied the Missionaries to the Prime Minister, who received them very courteously, and expressed himself much gratified at their arrival. He inquired about the respective branches of improvement which they would endeavour to promote among the people. He also intimated his wish to give Dr. Davidson a house for his residence, and another house close by for an hospital, and to render him every possible assistance in his work. We thanked him for his kindness, and when we left, he sent his aide-de-camp with us to show us the premises, which consisted of a spacious court or compound, now occupied by the houses of the minister's dependents, which, he said, would be cleared for the erection of a house and offices for the doctor. The site and space appeared most eligible. The residence is in the midst of a dense population, easily accessible to the Missionaries, and also of the chief nobles. I cannot but feel grateful to the Most High for this fresh evidence of His favour towards the Mission.

"Next day, after the King had read in the Bible, Mr. Toy, who had accompanied me, and who is acquainted with singing by notes, exhibited his books, and the modulator, or key to the new mode of singing on Mr. Curwen's plan. He explained the method of notation, and sung several new tunes. The King sent for his best singers, and they were all delighted with the simplicity and distinctness of the new mode. The King expressed his wish that Mr. Toy should come and live near him, and be the minister of Ambohipotsy, and that Mrs. Toy should teach the girls needlework, &c.

"On the 6th, Mr. Stagg, who had been ill with the fever, came to see my school, and was pleased with the attention and attainments of the pupils. I afterwards introduced him to the King, who made many inquiries about the progress of education in England, and seemed interested in the accounts of the efforts to raise the education of females and promote the welfare of women by extending the range of their occupation. He showed Mr. Stagg the school-house, built of stone, where his band was practising on the instruments sent from England. I have learned that the King is prepared to give orders for school-houses to be erected in the villages of the province, and to extend education as widely and rapidly as possible."

Although the Missionaries newly arrived at the capital were incapable of forming a just estimate of much that met their observation, the first impressions of one of them, given in a letter to a friend, deserve a record. It had been arranged that the young brethren should, shortly after their arrival, partake of the Lord's Supper with the united Churches of Antananarivo. "When we got there," writes the Missionary, "the place was crammed. The whole service was deeply impressive. The usual passages of Scripture were read, and Mr. Ellis and the several pastors exhorted the people, and prayed. The singing was heart-stirring and beautiful, very different from what you hear at home. Every one sung, and at the same time you could not help feeling that they were making melody in their heart to God." Mr. Ellis, referring to the same deeply affecting service, writes, "There appeared to be about eight hundred present. A great part of them were neatly, some of them tastily dressed in clean European and native dresses, and their calm, quiet, cheerful aspect was deeply affecting. More than once during the service, I was almost overcome by my feelings, especially when I reflected that little more than thirty (forty) years before, there was not a single believer in Christ—scarcely a single hearer of His Gospel. I could not help exclaiming more than once to the Missionaries, 'What hath God wrought!" They were all much affected, and said that they never expected to witness such a sight in Madagascar, and that they had never seen so many communicants together in England."

In a letter of a previous date, Mr. Ellis makes the following reference to the state of the Churches. "While writing this letter, I have had a visit from sixteen or eighteen pastors and officers of the Churches, who came to bring me a statement of the communicants, &c. They remained about two hours, in conference on the state of the Churches, and some of the difficulties arising from polygamy, &c. I wish the friends of Missions could have heard their account of the purity of the Church, and the standard of personal piety kept up amongst them. They would have exclaimed, 'It is the Lord's doing,' and would have taken fresh courage in their work; but I can only say that, though *the returns are incomplete*, they state the number of communicants to be *Seven hundred and forty*, and the number of Christians in the island to be *Seven Thousand.*"

In a subsequent communication, Mr. Ellis mentions another circumstance, which, though of a very different character from that which has just been described, illustrates the feelings of the Christians. "On the arrival of General

L.

Johnstone and the other officers of the Embassy," he writes, "the Christians came to ask me to go with them to pay what they considered a suitable mark of respect to the General. On reaching the place, I found a fine fat ox standing near the door, which they had brought as a present. I explained their object to the General, and when, accompanied by the Bishop of Mauritius and Captain Anson, he appeared at the verandah, Rainimarosandy stepped forth from among the native pastors and other Christians who formed a crowd in front of the house, and in a brief, sensible speech, expressed, on behalf of the Churches of the capital, the great satisfaction which the arrival of the General and his companions from England, the land of their earliest friends, had afforded them. He said they felt, after the kindness shown to them, that they were regarded as friends, and were bound by new ties to their brethren in England. That, following the customs of their country, they had brought the present of an ox (to which he pointed), and of which they begged his acceptance, as an expression of their gladness in seeing their friends and the friends of Radama amongst them. The General made a very appropriate acknowledgment, to which the Bishop added some equally appropriate remarks, both which I interpreted, and the parties then separated with mutual pleasure. There were many men of rank among the Christians present, who had worn the heavy chain in prison and in exile, who had drunk the tangena, who had been doomed to death themselves, or had lost, for their faith in Christ, their dearest earthly relatives, and there was on this, as on all similar occasions, a reality and heartiness in their words and demeanour that seemed to make a deep impression on the minds of the visitors, even on those that made no pretence to religion."

We close this illustration of the character and circumstances of the Christians by the following extract from the same communication; "I can only state that everything connected with the progress of religion, is, considering all the circumstances, most encouraging. I hear of scarcely any defections among the Christians from the integrity and purity of the Gospel, or any abatement in their zeal and earnestness in bringing others to Christ. Their numbers continue to increase, and the most marvellous and gratifying accounts are received from distant provinces."

The reference in the last paragraph is to a singularly interesting and important communication which has reached the capital since the Queen's death. It came from a part of the island, about 200 miles distant, to which some of the Christians were banished during the early period of persecution, who carried with them the precious truths for the faith and love of which they suffered. But though themselves "prisoners in bonds," they soon found that "the Word of God was not bound." Out of the fulness of their hearts, their mouths spoke of Christ and His salvation. What has been the result? " A wide and glorious harvest," writes Mr. Ellis, " invites the reapers to the field. * * *I am informed that there are thousands of believers in the Betsileo country."* Nor is this the only remote region, in which fruits of Christian effort have been matured during the darkness which has now passed away. In a postscript to a recent letter occur the following pregnant and suggestive words. " I received a visit from another party of Christians far to the south on the east coast. *The Hova officers at the military post have been the evangelists.*"

Such "marvellous and gratifying" revelations of the previously unknown and unanticipated effects of Christian influence in the more remote parts of Madagascar, concurring with the fact that in the capital the "numbers continue to increase," justify large expectations. Nevertheless the friends of Missions should "rejoice with trembling." One period of great trial has indeed passed, but another may be at hand. Prosperity may prove more fatal than persecution—the sunshine than the storm.

> " E'en more the treach'rous calm we dread,
> Than tempests bursting o'er our head."

And added to the enervating influences to which Christians have too frequently yielded when they have obtained rest from adversity, there are active and hostile agencies at work which must be regarded with vigilance and resisted with energy. It is well known that as soon as the country was open, a strong body of Catholic priests and Sisters of Charity hastened to the capital. These enemies of the truth will do their utmost to sow tares amongst the wheat, and they will succeed unless the friends of Protestant Christianity labour earnestly to counteract their influence. Thus only can the mischief be prevented.

But in this way it may be done, for, happily, the Bible was in Madagascar before the priest, and, when read and pondered, loved and preached as it is by the Malagasy, that blessed book is "mighty through God" against the subtleties and sophistries of Rome. The testimony, therefore, of Father Jouen, that "the whole Christianity" of the Malagasy "consists in reading the Bible," rightly interpreted, is an evidence of the success of Protestant labours, an indication of the source and simplicity of the piety of the people, and a ground for hope that they will not be turned away from the truth of God to mere forms and fables. And this hope is confirmed by the spirit of enquiry, the desire for instruction, and the full recognition and free exercise of the right of private judgment which prevail in Madagascar. The first act of Radama II. was to found an educational institute, and that has been followed by other measures designed to promote the general enlightenment of his subjects. It is true, indeed, that the priests of Rome, when unable to prevent, are skilled in perverting agencies contrary to their designs. This they have done, and will continue to do in Madagascar. Nevertheless, in the awakened intelligence, the enquiring spirit, and the scriptural education of the people, they and their system will have to contend with influences alike adverse and powerful. It will be a struggle between the dark night and the opening day; between irrational dogmas and dead forms, and the free spirit and vital power of evangelical truth. How widely these favourable influences are likely to extend may be inferred not only from what has already been stated, but from the following statement of Mr. Ellis.

"The schools require our immediate attention. Mr. and Mrs. Toy, as well as Mr. Stagg, have, in compliance with the earnest entreaties of the people, made a commencement, but we have the wants of the nation to provide for; and next to the preaching of the Gospel and the work of God's Holy Spirit on the hearts of the people, we feel that the efficiency of our labours and their permanent fruits will depend on the extent to which we may be able to impart thorough Scriptural and general education to the three or four millions who are looking up to us for instruction.

"The heads of the nation, especially the King, fully accord with us in these views. The first work of Radama on ascending the throne was not to build a fortress or a palace, but a substantial stone edifice to be used as a school, probably to become the germ of a high school or college. The King has since his coronation expressed his readiness to encourage the erection of schools in those parts of Imerina in which they existed in the days of Radama I. But we have a more extensive field to occupy now than that which was open in his day; we must, if possible, have schools at some of the ports on the coast, and there are places in the centre of the island, two hundred miles some of them from the capital, whence messengers have repeatedly arrived in search of books, and teachers or schoolmasters; and at one of these stations at least there are said to be thousands of Christians. We shall send them books; I shall if possible visit them, and am not without hopes of beginning the evangelization of the whole province of the Betsileo by leaving with them a native preacher and a schoolmaster. This is only the aspect of one province, others seem equally prepared for instruction; and it may serve to illustrate the desire of the Chiefs to further the work to state that on the day after I had informed the Prime Minister that the books, &c., were remaining at Tamatave for want of bearers, he sent off one of his aides-de-camp to Tamatave, with orders to secure and bring up at his own expense, or by his own servants, a case of Scriptures and a case of school materials for the use of his own people on his estates.

"Urgent as the appeals are which daily come to us to receive pupils or to open schools, I believe that we are but imperfectly acquainted with the extent to which God has by the events of His providence, and we hope also by the influence of His Spirit, prepared the Malagasy of the capital and the provinces to desire instruction, and seek after that knowledge which maketh wise unto salvation. We are also greatly encouraged by the readiness which the best among the Christians manifest to co-operate with us in this work. Our great hopes for its stability and permanency are drawn from the number of young persons already enrolled amongst the Christians, and from their great desire after instruction. All that we have any of us been able to do yet has been to teach English, for the use of the English language is already greater than we had expected to find it, and every spirited and intelligent

youth in the country seems anxious to learn our language. We could well employ a thoroughly qualified and pious master in teaching English only, but we fear the means of the Society will not allow you to send us one. We are glad, however, to know that among the materials already sent there are a number of English educational books. Spelling and easy reading-books seem to be most wanted just now, as a proof of which I may mention that the children of the nobles in my school had only three old books among them all. The strong partiality cherished by all classes for the English people doubtless increases their desire to obtain a knowledge of our language, and we cannot but rejoice in this, as tending greatly to promote friendly intercourse between themselves and us, but more especially as opening to them the rich treasures of experience and wisdom contained in our language. * *
We hope the friends of education in England will generously help us to meet the large and gratifying demand which Madagascar now makes upon our attention, and efforts to place within their reach the means of education and mental improvement. The entire country—now ruled by a monarch of rare liberality and humane desire for the enlightenment of his people—is open to the Christian teacher, who would be welcomed in every province of the island, and would be encouraged by the authorities. The Christians will do what they can in combination with our efforts, but after nearly thirty years of severe persecution, in which property, liberty, and life itself was often sacrificed, their means are in almost every instance exceedingly

limited. Whatever aid we may receive will be increasingly serviceable if received soon, for we are not the only teachers in the field, though the only teachers of the lessons of the Bible."

But while the confidence that, with the Divine blessing, the agencies now at work will powerfully impede, if they do not absolutely prevent the spread of popery in Madagascar, may reasonably moderate our fears, should the friends of truth be induced to relax their exertions in any degree, the evil consequences cannot but be serious. For it must not be forgotten that great multitudes of the people are still heathen, ignorant, depraved, and addicted to some of the lowest and worst forms of superstition. Even in the capital, the Christians do not constitute a fifth part of the population, and, with the exception of a few districts, the entire country is much as it was at the commencement of Missionary operations. Here, then, there is a state of society favourable for the priest. The supernatural pretensions and pompous ceremonial, the tinsel and trumpery of Rome are well adapted to attract those whose mental powers have not been quickened by the light of truth, and in whom the dominion of sense and imagination is almost absolute. With a field to act upon so wide and well prepared, especially in those parts where undisturbed night still broods, it surely could not awaken surprise, should the enemy sow tares amongst the wheat. If he fails to do so, it will not arise from deficient skill or energy. Success will assuredly reward the attempt of the Jesuits now in Madagascar, if subtle artifice, plausible falsehood, bold and almost blasphemous pretensions, and assiduous labour can command it. They will be aided, moreover, by the influence of the men who sought to effect a revolution in favour of France—an influence which it would be worse than folly to despise.

These considerations may be connected with the fact that, while popery is Protæan, and ready to vary its aspects and modify its requirements so as to meet the multiform circumstances and prejudices of those whom it seeks to proselyte, the system is nevertheless what it professes to be, unchanged and unchangeable, in this at least —that it ever and everywhere ministers to some of the deepest corruptions of human nature, and thus seeks to enlist fallen man under its banners. If, then, the friends of enlightenment and evangelization have to grapple with such a foe as popery, and to win for Christ a domain so wide and glorious as Madagascar, few agents, feeble efforts, and restricted means will not avail.

But if the proceedings of Romanists may awaken some solicitude, experience abundantly proves that their own reports of success should not be received until confirmed by better evidence. Repeatedly the most unfounded rumours, calculated to cast a shadow upon the prospects of Madagascar, and upon the character of its sovereign, have reached this country through Bourbon and France, which have shaken the confidence, and for a brief season have excited the fears of some of the friends of Protestant Missions. But perhaps the worst fabrication of this kind which has yet appeared, is a letter printed in the "Annals of the Propagation of the Faith," from Radama II. to the Pope, soliciting the prayers and blessing of His Holiness.

The professed object of this communication was so contrary to the known sentiments of the King, its style so obviously that of an adept in such servile compositions, and the fact that, while attributed to Radama, it was not subscribed with his name, were circumstances so suspicious, that by many it was thought to be a clumsy forgery. This conjecture has recently become certainty. We now learn that this document was actually forwarded to Rome, and that the Pope himself has been made the dupe of the Jesuit. In his simplicity, therefore, His Holiness despatched a reply to the King, with his autograph signature, which was translated and delivered. On receiving it Radama was amazed, and immediately denied the authorship of any letter to which it professed to be a reply. How far this pious fraud will advance the design of its author may be easily conjectured. The character both of the sovereign and of his subjects has been much misunderstood, if a resort to devices so unworthy does not augment the difficulty which the Catholic priest compared to that of " cutting a rock with a razor."

As an important means of propagating the truths for which the martyrs of Madagascar died, and commending their faith and heroism to their countrymen, the King has given the consecrated spots upon which they suffered, as sites for four large memorial Churches, and one of smaller size, and Mr. Ellis has apppealed to the friends of Missionaries in this country for the means of accomplishing this most interesting and important object. Apart from their commemorative character, these places of worship are urgently required. Mr. Ellis says that it is "their most pressing want at the present moment." But thus to glorify God in those who laid down their lives for His cause was a proposal which Mr. Ellis says, "pleased the King and the nobles, and greatly encouraged the Christians; and," he adds, "orders were immediately given that the pieces of land should be reserved for that special purpose, and his Majesty has, since my arrival, assured me that the ground shall be used for no other purpose, and shall be given to us whenever we require it." The names of the sites thus set apart will be familiar to the readers of these pages, Ambohipotsy, Arapimarinana, Faravohitra, Ambalinakanga, and Fiaduna. Sanctuaries upon these spots would, in Mr. Ellis's judgment, "provide admirably for the accommodation of the inhabitants of the principal portions of the city." The estimated cost of these erections—in a plain style, and of durable materials, each to accommodate from eight hundred to a thousand persons—is £10,000. Towards this the Christians of Madagascar will do all they can, although twenty-six years of spoliation and suffering have greatly reduced their means. "But," asks Mr. Ellis, "will England give to Madagascar these Memorial Churches, and thus associate the conflicts and triumphs of the Church with the remembrance of the source from which, through Divine mercy, Madagascar received the blessings of salvation, and thus perpetuate the feelings of sympathy and love which bind the Christians of Madagascar to their brethren in England?"

Cordially approving this proposal, and believing that it deserves the most generous support of every section of the Christian Church, the Directors have wisely addressed their appeal not only to their own more immediate constituents, but to all the friends of Evangelical Missions. The result has shown that their confidence was well founded. Already more than half the amount has been contributed, and they believe that from an object so truly Catholic and Christian, what is still required will not be withheld.

As the coronation of Radama II. marks the close of a period in the history of Madagascar, the crimes and cruelties of which have been faintly sketched in these pages, while it opens a new era, which justifies the hope that if the friends of Christ prove faithful to their trust, its progress in all that exalts a nation will be great and rapid, a description of that national solemnity will fitly close this volume. It is from the pen of Mr. Ellis, whose disinterested and inappreciable services, both to the Government and to the people of Madagascar, will give to his name a high and honorable place in its future history. Under date of September 23rd, 1862, he thus writes:—

"After a night of short sleep I rose, and soon after six, a captain and twenty men, in uniform and armed, came to my house, and drew up in front of the door. The officer said they were sent to conduct me to Mahamasura, the place in which the coronation was to take place, and to attend upon me through the day, and see that I was not incommoded by the people.

"When ready, I seated myself in my palanquin, with the star of the Order of Radama II., with which his Majesty had honoured me, and proceeded with my attendants through the city. In the latter part of my way, I was immediately behind the idols, and at one time quite surrounded by them; and at that early hour, hundreds of people, in palanquins and on foot, were pressing toward the entrance to the ground. Banners inscribed with "R. R. II.," were fixed on both sides of the road, at intervals of about every hundred yards; and tall green plantain-trees, had, during the previous day, been brought from the adjacent gardens, and planted, in groups of five or six together, by the side of the way. On the ground, the position assigned to the respective divisions of the people were also designated by banners bearing their names. Banners were also placed along the whole line of the platform.

"About half-past ten I took my place in front of the Christians, among the native pastors, on the south side of the steps leading to the throne, it having been agreed that we were to offer prayer at the time of the crown being placed on the head of the King. Although the Christians occupied more space than that allotted to them, more than half their number could not find admission to the ground. On the opposite side of the steps, were the Sisters of Charity, and about forty girls and children, and, still nearer the stage, five or six Catholic priests, and some of their people.

Immediately in front of the Sisters of Charity and the priests, were the idol-keepers, with their also small number of adherents. The idols, thirteen in number, were carried on tall slender rods or poles, about ten feet high. In most of them, there was little resemblance to anything in heaven or in earth; yet such were the objects on which the security and prosperity of the realm were formerly supposed to depend, and for refusing to worship which so many of the most intelligent and worthy among the people had been put to death, while others had been subjected to banishment, slavery, torture, fetters, and imprisonment!

"The stage or platform was occupied by members of the royal family on one side, and foreign guests on the other. Nearest the throne sat Rasalimo, the Sakalava princess, whose marriage with the first Radama was the seal of peace between the Sakalavas and the Hovas. Next to her sat one who in her day must have been one of the brightest belles in Madagascar, for traces of beauty still lingered in her oval face and expressive features. She had been the wife of the first Radama's father. The types of three successive generations of Malagasy nobles were there assembled, and it was deeply interesting to watch their varied aspects, the resemblance and the deviations from the Hova type, the latter being much fairer than any others.

"Some of the men were exceedingly handsome, among whom were the young Prince Ramonja, and Rambosalama's princely son. All were most gorgeously attired; scarlet was the predominant colour, though some wore green, others puce-coloured velvet. The gold lace, though not lacking, was not so abundant on the new as on the old uniforms. My scholars, sons of the nobles, in their velvet and gold uniforms, stood by my side, in front of the pastors, before the great body of the Christians.

"Before twelve, the clouds of dust, and denser throng in the road, as well as the firing of cannon along the mountain side, announced the approach of their Majesties. The Queen, splendidly attired in a white satin dress, and a tasteful ornament of gold on her head, rode first, in a scarlet and gold embroidered palanquin, accompanied by her adopted little girl, the child of Prince Ramonja's eldest daughter. The King rode beside her, mounted on a beautiful little Arab horse, and greeted by the plaudits of the joyous multitude, who crowded every available spot within sight of which the pageant had to pass; while the voices of the Christians might be heard singing most heartily the National Anthem, or Malagasy 'God Save the Queen.'

"Guards clothed in green, and bearing silver halberts, attended the royal pair, and the officers of the Missions from England and France, as well as other foreigners, and Malagasy officers of State, followed. The Queen ascended the flight of steps leading to the seats prepared for their Majesties, under the canopy erected over the *sacred stone* on which the monarch, on commencing his reign, exhibits himself to the heads of the nation. The King followed, wearing the British field-marshal's uniform presented by Her Majesty Queen Victoria, and a splendid light-coloured robe. The dresses of the officers of State were most of them new, and some of them gorgeous. The robe of the minister of justice was of green velvet, trimmed with gold lace, the train carried by two bearers. When their Majesties had been seated a few minutes, the King rose, and taking the crown from a stand on his right, placed it on his head. The firing of cannon announced the fact. The band struck up the National Anthem, while the multitude saluted the newly-crowned monarch with the Malagasy salutation, 'May you live a thousand years!'

"The King then turned to the Queen, who stood by his side, and taking a smaller open-work crown of gold from the page who bore it, placed it on the head of Her Majesty. After standing a minute or two, to receive the greetings of his officers, and the shoutings of the multitude, the King took off the crown, the Queen sat down, and the King then delivered his kabar or speech to the people, assuring them that his confidence in and affection towards them, and that his purposes for the welfare of his country and the prosperity of all classes, were the same as when he was raised to the throne, &c., &c. After this speech, of which I shall hereafter send a correct copy, the King resumed his seat, when we all presented the hasina —mine for the Missionaries and myself.

"I then retired, asking an officer in blue velvet and gold to accompany me to my tent.* I threw my photographic blouse over my dress, prepared and placed my plate in the

---

* Mr. Ellis had previously been requested by the King to take a photographic representation of the scene.

camera, and waving a white handkerchief as a signal, the King and Queen rose and walked to the front of the pavilion, and after a short interval I returned the signal that it was done. Their Majesties then resumed their seats, and the high officers continued to present their hasina. I proceeded to develop my picture, which turned out very well, so far as the chief objects were concerned. These, and part of the city, which formed the background, came out well. The constant moving of the multitude in front made the nearer objects confused, but this may be corrected and made complete by filling in the figures in the foreground from a second which I took.

"When their Majesties retired, the scene became more crowded than before. I saluted the King as he passed near my tent on his return, and was surprised at the quietness of his horse among the floating of banners, sounds of music, shouting of multitudes, and report of cannon; to say nothing of the shouting, and running to seek palanquins or bearers, as the vast multitudes, like a surging torrent, approached the place of exit from the ground to the road leading back to the palace.

"And now the scene—which, favoured by the nature of the country, a cloudless sky, and tropical sun, together with the joyous occasion which had produced it, made it one of the most imposing I had ever witnessed—began to change. The lower line of the granite mountain on which the city stands—and which two hundred feet above the plain, stretched from north to south behind the platform, at a distance of two or three hundred yards—had been thronged with spectators. Greater numbers still had spread themselves over the sides and summits of the hills to the north and the west; while a multitude was seen in beautiful perspective extending from the base to the very summit of Ambohi Zanahary (village of God), a massive circular hill to the south-west. This throng of spectators, clothed in the long flowing lambas of pure white, or deep rich glowing colours, and who, except when clapping their hands or shouting for joy, had been quiet gazers on the scene, were now seen moving in various directions until they were absorbed in the multitudes that crowded the roads leading from the plain.

"I had noticed as the King approached that the members of his family, especially those connected with the first Radama and his father, turned their faces towards him and clapped their hands, and sang some of the native songs, as was the custom in ancient times.

"I now packed up my camera, took down my tent, and made the best of my way home. The heat had become intense, especially in the small tent, and I was glad of some refreshment, having been on the ground from seven until nearly three. But before I had changed my dress a messenger came from the palace to say that the company were all assembled, and I therefore hastened to the coronation banquet, which was held in the large palace of Manjakamiadana.

"So far as choice, variety, and abundance were concerned, it was a right royal banquet. The silver-gilt goblets and tankard presented by Queen Victoria, very appropriately graced the upper end of the table where their Majesties sat, supported by the chiefs of the French and English Missions. The table was spread for a hundred guests, and that number actually sat down to partake of the royal bounty. A calf roasted whole and garnished, was the principal dish at the upper end. On the sideboards were piled large substantial portions of solid food; while poultry, game, and fish covered the table, which was ornamented with vases of silver, manufactured by native artists, after European models. There were ranged along the centre, with artificial flowers and sweetmeats, preserved apricots, and pine-apples, with plums and cakes intervening. The healths of the Sovereigns of Madagascar, England, and France, were drunk, with a few others, after one of which the King rose, drew his sword, and made an energetic speech as to the principles upon which he would exercise his authority, and which he considered would tend to the good or the injury of the country. Soon after sunset, the Missionaries and myself retired."

Other pens have recorded the transactions of that day, but they add little to the description of Mr. Ellis. There is, however, one point not named by him, to which a brief reference must be made. It appears—and the source of the statement may be surmised by those who are acquainted with men and things at the capital—that, when he crowned himself, Radama coupled the will of the European governors with that of God. But one of the most intelligent and influential witnesses of what occurred, who occupied a place on the dais close behind the Queen's chair, has emphatically contradicted this rumour. After placing the crown upon his own head, and upon that of the Queen, " he advanced," writes this gentleman, " drew his sword, and addressed the people in a spirited and stirring speech, which appeared to elicit unqualified approbation. As at the time this speech was much talked of I made particular enquiries about it, and am enabled, on the testimony of the most trustworthy Hova nobles, and some most intelligent and educated Malagasy *gentlemen*, not Hovas, whom all then at Antananarivo well knew as high class men, to give a flat contradiction to the statement that he ever mentioned in it that he was King by the will of God, and the *consent of the European powers*. What he did say was to the following effect. He was now King of Madagascar, *not because he had tried to be so* (a phrase evidently pointed at the reports so industriously circulated by some parties, and even printed, accusing him of being privy to several conspiracies against his mother, the late Queen), *but because God had willed it*, and that he intended to govern his people with kindness and justice. That such as they had found Prince Rakoto, merciful, tender of shedding blood, and ever solicitous of enlightening his country and advancing its material interests, so they would find him now as Radama II. Such a declaration would indeed touch the hearts of the dense multitude around him, so long and so cruelly oppressed in former times."

The facts recorded in these pages need no comment. They stand forth distinct and conspicuous either in their own bright light, or in unrelieved and appalling darkness. Never did the great Destroyer strive more strenuously or with less success than he has done to retain his long undisturbed dominion over the millions of Madagascar, and never did he find instruments more ready to execute his pleasure than in that habitation of cruelty.

On the other hand, Christianity was never more conspicuous, faith never more triumphant, and the presence and power of the Divine Spirit never more manifest than there. And surely such success should enlarge expectation and stimulate effort in the friends of Christ. As it was with the Churches of Judæa, and Galilee, and Samaria when they had rest, so should it be with the Churches of Madagascar, " Walking in the fear of the Lord and in the comfort of the Holy God," they should be " multiplied." And this is our hope concerning them. But much is demanded from us in order to its realization. We must "pray without ceasing." Prayer prevailed for the persecuted. Let it be as prevalent on behalf of the prosperous. But true prayer, while it is "power with God," has no less power "with men." It gives heart and energy to action, and sends forth the Christian worker from his closet to his work "in the strength of the Lord God." And never were these agencies more needed than now for the service of God in Madagascar. He has signally honoured the London Missionary Society in making it the instrument for the commencement of that great spiritual revolution which His own Almighty hand so gloriously sustained and spread after His servants had been driven from their post. And doubtless now that the field of labour is again opened, upon that Society the duty of cultivating it to the fullest possible extent, clearly devolves. For this the Directors are prepared. Six Missionaries are already at Antananarivo, in addition to their veteran friend Mr. Ellis, and four others will speedily follow them. But far more than this is required for such a land. This should be the settled conviction of every Christian heart, and when it is the work will be done. "Hasten it, O Lord, in thine own time!" "Come Lord Jesus, Come quickly!"

www.ingramcontent.com/pod-product-compliance
Lightning Source LLC
Chambersburg PA
CBHW020303170426
43202CB00008B/479